KIERAN MERVYN

Signs from Cara and Beyond

Messages from the Spirit World

First published by Independent Publishing Network 2022

Copyright © 2022 by Kieran Mervyn

All rights reserved. No part of this publication may be reproduced, stored or transmitted in any form or by any means, electronic, mechanical, photocopying, recording, scanning, or otherwise without written permission from the publisher. It is illegal to copy this book, post it to a website, or distribute it by any other means without permission.

Kieran Mervyn asserts the moral right to be identified as the author of this work.

Kieran Mervyn has no responsibility for the persistence or accuracy of URLs for external or third-party Internet Websites referred to in this publication and does not guarantee that any content on such Websites is, or will remain, accurate or appropriate.

First edition

ISBN: 978-1-80049-150-2

Cover art by Ray Brennan www.raybrennancreative.com
Cover art by Pierce Brennan

This book was professionally typeset on Reedsy.
Find out more at reedsy.com

This book is dedicated to people of all faiths and religions affected by brain disease. It's what Cara would have wanted.

"Amazing! Such a strong energy. Are you and your mum mediums, or is this the first experience you have had? I'm a medium and growing up would see visions like on your [Instagram] page e.g., on the curtains and walls. Lucky for me my mummy is also a medium so she knew what I was seeing".

Rosie Walsh, Psychic Medium, Ireland in communication with the authors (Dr Kieran and Faye Mervyn).

Contents

Foreword	iv
Preface	vii
Acknowledgement	ix
1 REVISITING IS MISE CARA	1
Grief (by Faye Mervyn)	3
2 RORY DARLEY (LEEDS) AMBASSADOR	5
3 STEPPING INTO CARA'S SHOES	7
To Daddy (by Faye Mervyn)	9
4 THIRD MEETING WITH LORNA BYRNE	11
5 SPIRITUAL MESSENGER FROM BELFAST	16
12th Birthday in Heaven	23
6 FINN WITNESSES THE AFTERLIFE	29
Bélmez Appearances in Spain 'La Casa de las Caras'	35
7 DARK SIDE	37
Fear (Faye Mervyn)	43
8 JIM HOGAN FROM CORK	45
9 A MIRACLE FROM HEAVEN	54
10 ALENA STEWART (SLOVAKIA)	58
Train Accident: Mind the Gap	63
Oracle Cards	64
The Phone Box	66
Lost and Found	66
The Feather (Faye Mervyn)	68
11 SIGNS FROM NIGERIA	70
Raheema and the Car Crash	76
Falls Road Knockdowns	77

Cara's Love of Animals	79
Mise Éire	80
Man that Stole the Leaf	81
12 LANA'S CANOE TRAGEDY (SOUTH AFRICA)	83
13 DAME JULIE IHEYINWA WOKOCHA (NIGERIA)	91
14 GRANDFATHER FROM MAYO	96
15 SIGNS FROM MARTIN (CANADA)	98
16 ASYA RIP JUNE 2022 [ISTANBUL]	107
POEMS	114
17 DION JUDE HUTCHINGS (NEW YORK)	117
Dion's Wake	120
Dion's Funeral	121
A Package from my Cousin	123
The Music Box	123
Camille (RIP)	124
Rose with Black Thorns	125
18 ANN'S SIGNS (AUSTRALIA/USA)	129
Synchronicity first impacting on Ann's Awareness.	130
Another Synchronicity	131
Ann meeting her husband	131
The Station Wagon	133
Ann's Father Passing	134
Ann's Mother Passing	135
St Margaret's York Shrine	138
Kieran at St Margaret's Shrine (Summer of 2022)	141
19 PENNIES FROM HEAVEN (BELFAST, IRELAND)	142
Figure akin to Our Lady	147
Cara's Pendant	147
Nana's Needle	148
20 INEZ SYLVIA JOHNSON (JAMAICA)	149
21 AN UNEXPLAINED COINCIDENCE (PAPUA NEW GUINEA)	156
22 THE LETTER ~ DEBBIE LAMOUR (IRELAND)	160

23	FLEUR ALANA & OTHERS (AUSTRALIA)	165
	'The Others'	168
	'Our' Fleur Alana	169
	Setting up a Family Burial Plot	173
	Strange Happenings	174
24	CARA'S PREMONITIONS (IRELAND/LEEDS)	179
25	THE CLOCK (MADAGASCAR)	182
26	CARA'S FUNERAL ANNIVERSARY	187
	Family Connections	189
	Cara's 14th Heavenly Birthday	190
27	CAMPBELL CLARK (LEEDS)	192
	Whistler	197
28	RECOGNITION FROM THE CHURCH	199
29	TERRY J. BOYLE (CANADA)	203
30	THE RING AT CLONARD MONASTERY	206
	Faith of the Gypsies	207
	Face on Television	207
31	NOTE FROM GRANNY MARIE (IRELAND)	209
32	TAYA (LEEDS)	212
33	VJOLLCA'S DAD (KOSOVAR-ALBANIAN)	214
34	AALIYAH – HIGHEST POWER (IRELAND)	219
35	SUMMARY ~ SIGNS FROM CARA AND BEYOND	227
36	IS MISE CARA BRAIN DISEASE FOUNDATION	235
37	ABOUT THE AUTHORS	239
38	LETTER TO AMMA (INDIA)	241
39	MARTY IMLACH (SCOTLAND)	247
40	MICHAEL MELVILLE (LIVERPOOL)	250
BIBLIOGRAPHY		252
About the Author		253
Also by Kieran Mervyn		254

Foreword

Claudia Rusenescu (Brain Tumour Patient and Is Mise Cara Brain Disease Foundation Trustee)

I want to express my gratitude and appreciation to the prolific authors of this book. They have wholeheartedly shared such vivid experiences. Reading this book has been a peculiarly sensory experience, a feast for all my senses, reinforcing my spiritual consciousness in unexpected ways with each chapter.

I started reading the current book late in July, sitting on my hammock chair in the garden one evening. I had an avid feeling of advancing my revelation that the previous book, 'Is Mise Cara: Orbs, Souls and Holy Ghosts,' engendered. What an emotional experience it's been! Crickets' chirping and fireflies' sounding became increasingly more intense, reverberant, and much more delightful than usual. It simply felt like amid a summer night fairy-tale, with a chorus accompanying my reading – I cannot describe how beautiful and special this was! My mom also observed this, noting that she cannot remember the last time the whole of nature was so finely tuned singing. She did not know what I was doing then, so I passionately believed something magical had happened that night.

This experience moved me to the core, as I felt this veil of love and protection from Cara transposed within mother nature. For a few seconds, I considered recording my thrilling experience. Still, then, I felt a sensation of deep gratitude that this is something spiritual, divine greatness unveiled to me through the book because of Cara's empowering, caring, and loving force.

The purest lesson I've ever had about meaningful synchronicities, in line with what Alena Stewart mentioned in Chapter 10: "In all synchronicities, what is important is not 'the objective facts of the coincidences, but the emotional impact they had on the people involved" (Robert Hopcke). This experience was so emotion-packed and stirring that I'll never forget it!

This book will change life perspectives, resonating with many people with similar experiences. Many people are not necessarily very open to exploring the higher realms of human experiences in their profound sense, although they might wish to. People like me sometimes get overwhelmed with mundane duties, which are evanescent at the end of the day. They pay little attention to timeless or spaceless spirituality.

This book revealed many moving stories that made me feel part of them. It enabled me to understand unique phenomena from different angles of synchronicity rather than telepathy (e.g., the process of receiving thoughts from another person); and to feel the magic of that initial reading in the garden.

On another note, I am a very optimistic young person with tremendous and valued personal and professional dreams. However, I was diagnosed with a brain tumour about five years ago, in my second year of my Bachelor of Engineering Studies. The doctors determined that after two seizure episodes, which occurred in quite challenging times juggling studies with work. Thankfully, I had my boyfriend alongside me in Hull while most of my family remained overseas, in my native Romania. I cannot tell how much I needed a short respite with loved ones to relax and re-assemble our forces to stand up to the unexpected condition keenly. God's love and support were unconditionally guarding me during these five years. I express my sincere gratitude for my overall health condition was steady and satisfactory. Yet, there were seldom psychological effects and agony that could be arduous to cope with, especially at a young age.

I am delighted to be part of Is Mise Cara Brain Disease Foundation Charity. There is a constant drive and firm belief that together we will bring about that needful change in research, diagnosis, and treatment of brain diseases. Our inceptive objectives involve empowering, restoring, and socially including people living with or affected by brain disease. We will provide opportunities for respite and family time. In the long run, we will further concentrate on national fundraising events and voluntary health sector talks, with donations to brain tumour support.

As a Trustee, I will dedicate my work towards raising awareness, supporting children and young people living with brain diseases, and funding novel research initiatives for better treatments and, ultimately, the long-sought cure!

Proceeds from the sales of *Signs from Cara and Beyond ~ Messages from the Spirit World* will support the Is Mise Cara Brain Disease Foundation

www.carabraindiseasefoundation.com

Preface

'Signs from Cara and Beyond' explores the concept of meaningful synchronicity. One may be open to the spirit world or attribute such phenomena to quirks of nature, flukes, accidents, coincidences, or pure luck. Synchronicity relates to the gap between the inner realm (the subjective reality of dreams and interpretations) and the external realm (an objective, measurable reality).

We (the authors and contributors) believe that supernatural and paranormal events that occur during periods of sorrow have real meaning or may contain veiled messages. The signs we share may stimulate curiosity about the afterlife, helping us to understand life beyond the rational realm and, by extension, our soul's purpose.

The NDERF.org website shares over 5000 testimonies about near-death experiences (NDEs) where people recount extraordinary out-of-body experiences. These include floating out of one's body and observing new realms, viewing their physical frames after critical accidents, engaging with ancestors and angel-like figures, and countless other vivid experiences. One such account from the NDERF.org website homepage states:

Something told me telepathically that this space was reserved for me. "One day, your essence, your spirit, your experiences, will find a home there. Nothing is ever be lost or destroyed. I promise you, all will work out fine in the end. There's No need to worry. But, you have plenty of things to be getting on with. So, go, live your life well."

I felt so much incredible love from this entity. The intensity of the love I felt from it is indescribable, and the bliss that I felt in myself beholding that was beyond ecstasy.

Royalties from this current book and our first publication, Signs from Cara and Beyond will support the *Is Mise Cara Brain Disease Foundation* www.carabraindiseasefoundation.com

Brain tumours are the biggest cancer killer in people under 40, yet it remains a significantly underfunded and under-researched domain. Our foundation will provide respite and support to families and raise funds and awareness for brain diseases.

Everyone involved in the production of this book is helping to lift the veil of the spirit world, opening doors to others who seek new dimensions of wisdom, knowledge, and enlightenment.

Acknowledgement

NOTE
OF APPRECIATION TO LORNA BYRNE &
Claudia Rusenescu (Romania)
Rory Darley– IMCBDF's First Ambassador (UK)
Margaret O'Driscoll (Ireland)
Alena Stewart (Ireland/Slovakia)
Benjamin Samuel (Nigeria)
Jeff Fielding (South Africa)
Jessica Ng (Canada)
Merve Duran (Turkey)
Linda Hutchings (New York)
Ann R. Neal (Florida)
Bridette Mawhinney (Ireland)
Rohan Johnson (Jamaica)
Charles Stevens (UK)
Jack Lamour (Ireland)
Jacqueline Hiddlestone (Australia)
Harigo Andre (Madigascar)
Sandra Campbell (UK)
Cara's Granny Marie Mervyn &
Aunt Donna Marie Mervyn (Ireland)
Sophia McCourt (UK)
Vjollca Behluli (Kosovo)
Lauren and Karl (Ireland)
Marty Imlach (Scotland)
Michael Melville (UK)
Mahesh Hariharan
Khalid and Yasemin Mukhtar
Ray and Pierce Brennan (Ray Brennan Creative)

Dr Kieran Mervyn
CEO IS MISE CARA BRAIN
DISEASE FOUNDATION

Faye Mervyn
CHIEF MARKETING OFFICER
IS MISE CARA BRAIN DISEASE
FOUNDATION

1

REVISITING IS MISE CARA

'Sorry – it's God speaking. He's changing the words as I speak' (Lorna Byrne's words when praying to Kieran and Faye).

Lorna Byrne uttered these words in 2021 as she prayed over us (see chapter on 'Lorna Byrne's Third Meeting' below). Lorna plays a central role in our first book 'Is Mise Cara: Orbs, Souls, and Holy Ghosts' (2020) (hereafter referred to as, 'Is Mise Cara'), where we share our experience after losing Cara at Christmas 2019.

The essence of this book is hope for everyone - and for humanity. For people to improve, become happier and more content, change, evolve, and feel at peace. Until then, Lorna believes that other things in the universe must develop as they are. God must continue to take souls like Cara home.

"Death is like birth; I know you might think that's a strange thing to say, but you are being born into a new life. You actually don't 'die', it's only this physical shell that you leave – like an empty eggshell." **(Lorna Byrne, Angels in My Hair)**

Cara Mia Mervyn was born early, at 29 weeks gestation. She experienced health problems that led to a tracheotomy and significant surgeries from a young age. She had a quirky accent and an even quirkier sense of humour, perhaps due to having parents from Belfast and Leeds. In the introduction chapter to *Is Mise Cara*, we describe the Leeds Irish connection and the great work performed by The Leeds Irish Centre that performs noble community work, e.g.

Supporting people with complex needs and helping to locate and engage older people who have lost touch with family. They specifically target the socially isolated - helping people to reconnect and feel part of a more extensive support network. So, the Leeds Irish connection with the historical name 'Cara' seemed a perfect fit. And as you will see, Cara was true to her name. She became incredibly passionate about the socially excluded, whether giving money or food to the homeless or buying products to support refugees.

As Cara aged, her lungs gradually started to function better after previously struggling to breathe. Things seemed to look up for Cara, yet we visited her consultant as she experienced dizzy spells when lying on her back. Unfortunately, from that appointment on, things went downhill. Cara had an MRI, and we learned that Cara had a brainstem tumour. It was devastating. The biopsy was so complicated that Cara almost didn't make it through the procedure. In the 18 months to follow, we crammed in as much fun and holidays as possible. The *Is Mise Cara* book exemplifies making the best of a bad situation and finding hope in turbulent times.

Grief (by Faye Mervyn)

I wake up in the night with a blast from the past, and all the old memories come flooding back.
I wipe away a tear that runs down my face, knowing that it's grief and here to stay.
It's as if I don't know whether to laugh or to cry. But I feel like I'm visited by a love that is mine.
I want to hold you, to have one more time and show the world that you are indeed mine.
I know that you're near and you won't let me go.
But my time is still here, and I guess I must stay, but I know we'll meet up in the clouds one day.

Fig.1 Cara Mervyn (designed by her brother Finn)

"I definitely feel loving energy from your [Instagram] page. [Cara] has such strong energy to get such clear signs through to you and let you all see she is still very much around ♥ My sister passed away 13 years ago and we still hear her pace the floor upstairs in my mummy's house; it brings such comfort x" (Rosie Walsh, Psychic Medium, Ireland)

2

RORY DARLEY (LEEDS) AMBASSADOR

This book has been written in the context of brain disease continuing to claim or affect the lives of many patients, old and young. In January 2022, we received devastating news from Rory Darley's wife, Rachel, that Rory had passed away after a long battle with brain cancer. Rory from West Yorkshire had agreed to be the First Ambassador for our new charity in memory of Cara.

Fig. 2 Rory Darley (RIP) with a copy of Is Mise Cara

3

STEPPING INTO CARA'S SHOES

Cara experienced multiple health challenges for almost 12 years, culminating in a brainstem tumour. She received saline nebulisers to help moisten the airway and paralysed vocal cords damaged after tracheal surgery. Occasionally, we administered steroid nebulisers (Budesonide) when her airway became inflamed due to chest and lung infections. Cara also needed repositioning and support through the night during bouts of stridor. We'd position her pillows at a certain angle and could tell when she deviated from this position. Her breathing would become gradually raucous and laboured.

Immediately after Cara's brainstem tumour diagnosis, we described in *Is Mise Cara* how we were permitted to travel abroad after receiving the biopsy results. It was bittersweet, but we were elated to take the kids to Majorca for a week. It took us some time to relax after sleepless nights of laying, watching Cara snuggle into Finn. Ruminating over the initial shock of the prognosis, we replayed the consultant's words about potentially having 'Many Many Years.' This forecast was related to a potential low-grade brainstem tumour diagnosis.

Fig. 3 Cara putting up a fight

Toward the end of the holiday, I experienced significant breathing problems.

Faye quickly administered budesonide medication through Cara's nebuliser. It was akin to being slowly choked to death. I watched Cara and Finn coalesce in a panic. Upon arrival at the medical centre, the manager directed Faye back to the hotel for insurance documents and my passport. Luckily, a clinician could administer a steroid injection and some pills. I remember thinking how frightening it must have been for Cara and others with similar, but long-term health problems.

To Daddy (by Faye Mervyn)

As I put pen to paper, what can I say? I know wee "Magoo" is looking our way.
She guides like an angel and spreads love around. Her image appears in all that is sound.
Her love for you so precious will always be found; she never lets you go and keeps her feet on the ground.
I know on your birthday, she will make your day and show you something special in her unique way.
The feathers and the orbs are all ours to keep, and we must remember this as we soundly sleep.
It's your birthday, so have a great day, "Magoo" loves her Daddy in a wonderful way!

Our first book also describes the last family visit to Belfast after a trip to Donegal. Shortly after Boxing Day, Cara was feeling unwell, so we postponed a trip to Belfast to see family. We had a great Christmas that year, and Cara had a ball. But early on the morning of December 29, she was found dead in bed after a seizure. We battled to resuscitate her for about 15 minutes. We believed we could save her but couldn't.

Lorna Byrne experienced a similar situation in relation to grief with her husband, Joe. She referred to Joe as a literal match made in Heaven. She grieved deeply but acknowledged God's wish for him to

return home. Lorna believes that souls returning to Heaven are all a part of our evolution.

4

THIRD MEETING WITH LORNA BYRNE

Lorna Byrne met with us for the third time in June 2021. The meeting concerned the growing body of supernatural visitors to our home and the pictures and videos we shared with Pearl and Lorna. Lorna didn't see this follow-up book on Meaningful Synchronicity as a particular priority. She described how the world needed healing and how we should work harder at promoting and distributing our first book, 'Is Mise Cara', more widely. Lorna greatly supported our work and took over a precious hour of her time discussing current events, the power of prayer, and our role in sharing messages of hope.

We discussed global warming, the ravages of war, and the afterlife in detail. She mentioned Cara's continued role in people's lives. How Cara was in the most special realm, and how we should pray to Cara to help souls here on earth. Lorna's demeanor differed from the previous two meetings (we previously shared how in the first meeting, she described meeting Cara in the afterlife). On several occasions, Lorna stopped us and reiterated the importance of our first book. We plan to translate and distribute the book more widely and share the stories and experiences with a bigger global audience.

Something incredible happened at the end of the meeting, which we shared with Pearl. Lorna has since permitted us to include it in the current book. The first surreal experience occurred as Lorna prayed over Faye and me. The words of this powerful prayer became distorted as Lorna prayed, and it seemed to take Lorna several minutes to complete what normally takes less than 30 seconds.

Prayer of Thy healing Angels (Lorna Byrne)

Knowing the prayer by heart, I opened my eyes on a few occasions when I heard Lorna change the words at different parts of each sentence. Using what seemed like old-fashioned and biblical terms, she went off on a tangent before returning to other parts of the prayer. Then off on a tangent again. She apologised, saying:

"Sorry – it's God speaking. He's changing the words as I speak".

I could feel an amazing presence as Lorna spoke. Her eyes dazzled, and she looked like she wasn't quite present. Lorna advises:

"This prayer is about the light of God's healing hand, but when you say this prayer, we receive the light of healing that comes straight from God. As God touches us with His hand, He surrounds us, at the same time, with His Healing Angels that comfort us in this prayer."

"God is letting us know that he has sent this prayer from Heaven with His most powerful angel of all, Archangel Michael. It is a powerful prayer. It reminds us that we must always remember to allow the healing to be whatever way God grants it."

When the prayer ended, she asked us to close our eyes as she delivered a second prayer. At this stage, Faye and I experienced what seemed like two different, out-of-body experiences. I shared this text with Pearl (copied from Faye's post to Lorna's Circle of Light Facebook page):

"Hi, Pearl. We'd a special experience when your mum prayed to us at the last meeting. God was changing her words as she spoke. I didn't want to discuss this without checking with Lorna first."

"Happy to share a piece now. 'Our daughter Cara Mia (RIP, 2019) appeared to Kieran in his mind's eye as Lorna prayed and took one [of his] hands. She was younger than her passing age, glowing in a white dress, and just smiled. Our Lady then appeared to his other side and took his other hand. She was much taller than Cara but also glowing - a beautiful colour of sparkling white. He described them as pure white, pure love, and pure peace. It was the most special blessing' X (Faye's Facebook message, 2021)."

Faye experienced what appeared to be a hand on her neck and was surrounded by warm air during Lorna's second prayer. Another magical experience. We discuss a similar experience later in this book e.g., at St Margaret's Shrine, York.

An interesting 'coincidence' occurred when a lady called Margaret began following the @caramiamervyn Instagram account after Faye liked one of her posts on the Lorna Byrne Instagram account. By a twist of fate, we realised that both families had experienced the recent loss of a child, and both had experienced signs from the other side.

5

SPIRITUAL MESSENGER FROM BELFAST

by Donna Marie Mervyn

"She was with Lily. She went to bed, took a turn, landed on a white bed [white hospital bed in LGI] and never came around. She heard her mum and dad squealing on the phone".

Fig. 5 Lily, sisters Mary and Mena

Lorna Byrne from the South of Ireland regularly communicates with the spirit world through her angels, being a non-commercial spiritual messenger. Lorna's messages from Cara (as discussed in *Is Mise Cara*) were something we never imagined could have been replicated. The level of detail was incredible. So, we were overwhelmed to receive a detailed summary of my sister Donna's visit to another well-respected spiritual messenger called Orlaith from the North of Ireland.

In September 2021, Orlaith and Donna met in Belfast. Orlaith began the reading by saying,

"Two people are with me now... one of them was someone who passed very suddenly". Orlaith asked:

"Who is Ellen Elizabeth Lily? This person is like a mother figure".
My Granny Lily, seen above with her sisters Mary and Mena, was a spiritual woman who attended daily mass and regularly prayed the rosary. Orlaith referred to the "young one who passed suddenly called Cara is with me" [our darling daughter Cara, RIP 2019].

Orlaith mentioned how Cara knows that she "rocked your world upside down" and how:

"Cara was taken from her parents when she fell asleep; she feels very young to me."

Orlaith sensed that it was due to something akin to an aneurysm [Cara had a seizure linked to a brain tumour]. She asked Donna if "someone had told her about me?" because Cara seemed to know herself.

"She is with Lily. She went to bed and took a turn and landed on a white bed and never came around. Cara told me that she heard her mum and dad squealing on the phone".

> *"She's telling me that she wasn't long at the big school and described the school uniform"* [colours and style from Cardinal Heenan High School].

> *"She's saying the name Margaret"* [Cara's Great Grandmother Margaret (RIP)].

> *"She's telling me she misses her mum, dad, and little brother so much."*

Orlaith then mentioned Cara's "white coffin and carriage" and continued, "She has so much love for her mammy, daddy, and family". Orlaith then asked if the 19th or 20th of December seemed familiar. She mentioned,

> *"My mummy didn't have me on New Year's Eve".*

My Granny Lily was Maltese and moved to Ireland as a young girl. She gave birth to my mother, Marie, on New Year's Eve in 1947. I was subsequently born on New Year's Eve, 1974.

> *"Who's Marie Theresa? Who's Lily? She's calling her".*

> *"Your mother is a quiet woman and is very hurt."*
> *"The older lady had a baby taken from her and is buried in Milltown Cemetery on the Falls Road."* [Marie Theresa is my mother, and I know Lily had several miscarriages].

Orlaith asked:

> *'Who is K'? She's asking for him and said that she wants her mummy and daddy to be happy and that she wanted to go to the big girl's school where she had friends."* [She often called me K (Kieran)].
> *"There's a baby boy with her; he's autistic (ADHD). Cara is going to help him. She's asking you to pray <u>to</u> her, for him, but don't pray <u>for</u> her".*

Lorna Byrne mentioned that the child we lost during a miscarriage was a boy who appears to us (as discussed in our first book, *Is Mise Cara*). Orlaith shared more fascinating messages:

"I see Fibromyalgia" [also called fibromyalgia syndrome (FMS), as a long-term condition that causes pain all over the body].

She mentioned how Paddy has crumbling bones. She then mentioned Paddy Joseph. Orlaith said,

"Cara is laughing; she says "... it's not Pat, it's Paddy". [My father, Paddy (Cara's Grandfather), is severely disabled].

Orlaith also asked 'Who is John?" Perhaps my Uncle John, an ex-soldier from the Irish army? He's in her thoughts and prayers.

"Faye and Kieran are the loveliest souls. All about family and friends". Tell Faye that Cara is OK. That she is with family. Please take comfort that she's loved beyond measure; she's actually skipping and dancing away here.

"She loved Bundoran." [Cara loved Donegal; her last trips to Ireland included there and Belfast before flying home].

Orlaith mentioned a *"problem with the house. You live beside the Royal Victoria Hospital".* Our grandparents live a few streets away. She asked: "who was diabetic?" and then mentioned how it was *"nothing to worry about."*

More names mentioned were Billy, Mary, Jennifer, Annie. There is no Billy in the family apart from Faye's cousin, but Mary could be Lily's sister.

Marie's sister, Lily (Lily's daughter), has a daughter called Jennifer. Annie may be my great-aunt Ann or my uncle Ray's sister-in-law Annie who passed away in December 2022).

Orlaith then asked, *"Who's Liz? Did she kill herself?"* There is no knowledge of Liz in the family, but many souls seem to visit our home, perhaps from different clans. Then "Who's Lisa"? She's thinking of her [My sister Lisa].

Orlaith continued how Cara's now thanking Donna for donating a kidney to her sister Carla (Cara's Aunts). Orlaith remarked, *"Someone had cancer and kidney trouble."* My sister, Carla, had both.

"Reece negative: rare blood group. Donna, you are a match. You helped her through it. She's fine now."

"Granny [Lily] has placed a red rose on your knee, Donna. She's just kissed you on the cheek and thanked you for what you did for Carla. Look out for a feather and someone with the name Rose. That's a sign".

We share a series of messages from Rosie Walsh (a Physic Medium from Ireland) who reached out to us in May 2022 with signs from Cara. The three Irish physics and spiritual messengers that shared messages with us [Orlaigh (Belfast), Rosie (Kerry), and Lorna (Kildare)] aren't known to one another as far as we know. Perhaps this message from Rosie Walsh was a sign that Orlaith was referring to?

what it is reminding me of. She shows me a memory of a family gathering that seems to be in a warmer country like Spain she shows me family gathered round a table outside. For some reason she keeps making me aware she is bare foot. I feel chest/heart pain but this is where Cara comes through stronger, she says she does not want to talk about pain, they are in no pain now. She shows me a group hug with her parents and brother and her and I feel the love she felt from her family. She is writing 'brother' and drawing a circle around

Excerpt from Rosie Walsh's Instagram correspondence with Kieran and Faye

Describing Cara, Orlaith mentioned how Cara was referring to the colour of her hair:

"I have dark hair but would love to be blonde."

"Cara is such a beautiful wee thing; those eyes are shimmering brightly. She's covered in gold."

"She's a very happy wee girl, talking in a Yorkshire accent." She says,

***"They are the kids you never got the time with"* [miscarriage]. She says her**

"wee brother Finn is six and how it was a nine upside down." "A song was playing, and she mentioned how she loved the song."

In another correspondence with Rosie Walsh, she mentioned:

"Just as I am reading this about your Da (who is in poor health), I hear Cara singing like 'oh Cara your the prettiest girl' it's like a made up song lol she's laughing at me trying to sing it back. Would her granda have sang this to her?" My da would often sing Abba songs including Mama Mia to Cara. Rose then remarked: *"That's funny, when I seen the image of Spain and the outside table I thought this looks like it's from mama Mia"* **(Rosie Walsh, 2022)**

Returning to Donna's reading with Orlaith, she then moved on to key happenings since Cara's passing. Her 12th birthday, and celebrating Christmas and Easter.

12th Birthday in Heaven

We assembled outside The Holy Name of Jesus Catholic Church in Otley Road, Leeds, for Cara's Heavenly birthday celebration just a month after she passed. Cara mentioned to Orlaith how:

"There was a guard of honour during my 12th birthday celebrations. I saw all my friends, and they were clapping and let go of my balloons. Tell them that I caught every one of them".

Fig. 6 Cara, aged 5, with Finn, Mum and Dad

Orlaith highlighted once more how Cara was such a beautiful child and how her "Eyes were shining so brightly." On Christmas, Cara referred to St Stephens Day (Boxing Day). She said:

"Don't let my passing destroy the Christmas pattern. Complete what was created".

Orlaith: "Who's Peter?" Cara then mentioned how 'Peter Rabbit' represented Easter [we did the Easter bunny run for Cara and Finn each year, and Cara would often watch Peter Rabbit as a kid).

Orlaith: "Whose birthday is around Easter"? (My sister Donna's is in April). She's saying:

"Happy birthday! I won't be able to speak to you for a while, so I'm saying Happy Birthday now."

Orlaith mentioned again how Cara was very happy and at peace and knew that her pictures were placed *"all over the house."*

Orlaith concluded: "She's thanking you for the Clonard mass and mammy and daddy's petition."

Cara says, *"Don't feel guilty; Lily came for me." "Cara's dancing away here."* She says, *"there's a wee boy dressed in pink." "Your granny (Lily) is bowed down before the chapel. She's congratulating them. Cara's clapping her hands."*
"Cara's the highest vibration of love. Gold is all around her, and her eyes shine brightly".

Kieran and Faye

We had similar conversations with Lorna Byrne about Cara and, in the first book, shared our direct experiences of witnessing supernatural phenomena in real time. Lorna refers to God's realm, Heaven, as simply magical, the realm that humans will never wish to leave. Lorna explained how when the soul leaves the body for Heaven, an overwhelming feeling of love, joy, peace, and relief permeates. Judging by the number of testimonies of near-death experiences and visions of the afterlife after accidents, many people have vividly described the experience of their souls leaving their bodies.

In one example by Carbone (2020), a London paramedic called Adam Tapp was 35 years old when he passed away and came back to life minutes later. He was one of the 158 participants in a study that used text mining and artificial intelligence [AI] to find that 'most people respond positively to near-death experiences or NDEs.'

Tapp was doing some woodworking in his shop on 28th February 2018 when he was electrocuted. His heart stopped for eleven and a half minutes. He was strenuously resuscitated and fell into a coma for six hours. Tapp didn't wake up for six hours, and when he did, he was in ICU, intubated, which is quite a strange way to wake up, according to him. But while he was essentially dead to the material world, he recounted withstanding a profound experience.

"All of a sudden, I just woke up in a place that seemingly I'd always been. It was black, and it kind of seemed like space", said Tapp. "I wasn't Adam, I wasn't a paramedic, I wasn't anything. It was just like this raw form of consciousness where I was just existing very happily and pleasantly". Tapp said he then felt a "frequency" wash over him and saw what looked like "gasoline on the water with all these geometric shapes and patterns," adding that something was communicating with him through "thoughts and feelings and emotions." "I just started fading into the fabric of the universe. It was so warm and peaceful and pleasant [i]".

Cara had similar experiences, e.g., after almost passing away during the brainstem biopsy in 2018. In the Chapter 'The God Spot' (see *Is Mise Cara*), we wrote:

> **'Cara's brainstem tumour opened our eyes to the brutal reality of this disease. I remember seeing Cara in anguish after her release from the hospital after the biopsy. Tiny samples of the tumour left a slight wobble in her eye. Her balance was off, and she looked to us in peril. As we sat on her bed, she asked me my age, and when I said "44", she paused and said: "well, you've only about 50 years left". I joked that "I'd be delighted to live until 94". Looking concerned, I asked her if everything was OK. She then told me about a dream where she had died during surgery and how she observed us both walking down the hospital corridor'.**

Our first book presents some of Cara's other premonitions, including one concerning her coffin. As discussed earlier, when Lorna Byrne crossed over with her child, the angels explained how it wasn't her time and why she had to return. This experience relates to one of our conversations with Lorna. I described a recent experience where a premature baby lay on Faye's belly as she slept. Face peeping from under the quilt. It was ultrabright but extremely small with a tiny little head. Lorna confirmed that it was our little boy who died during a miscarriage. Cara often appears to the family in dreams holding a small child's hand, and she continues to visit family members.

We take great pleasure in knowing that Cara is active and remains very close to home. Cara's soul burns brightly because of a lifetime of health problems, concluding with the brainstem tumour. Cara was so pure and ultra-kind. And extremely emotionally intelligent. We asked Lorna if Cara's purpose continued in the afterlife. We presumed that souls appearing around our home and beyond were lost, and needed prayers, but Lorna explained that this wasn't the case. It's people on Earth who need prayers. We are privileged to have such experiences, which continue in different forms. However, some of the faces of (lost?) souls don't always appear so kind or positive.

Lorna continues to guide us and advises how to deal with it all – good and bad. Prayers are essential. Cara continues to enter our dreams at times in the most vivid ways. It often seems like she's guiding us from danger. On 15th November 2022, I woke to see a large dark menacing shadow floating above our bed between Faye and me. As I reached out, I heard what seemed like a small explosion which Faye slept through. It seemed like a clash of the physical and spirit worlds.

I turned my back, closed my eyes, and prayed for the Archangel Michael to protect the family and the house from evil. Lorna doesn't like to mention his name. When confirming seven Amazon keywords for the advertising of *Is Mise Cara,* **we noticed 666 competitors for our keyword 'heaven movies.' Perhaps someone somewhere loathes the positive energy emerging through the book and follow-up activities promoting healing and hope for many people.**

Cara's Friends in Cara's Granny's Garden

When visiting Manchester in August 2021, I dreamt that a large, powerful, and sinister figure was outside the hotel window. Lots of people appeared around him, requesting his help. He looked confident and mentioned having many resources to help people in different ways. Then little souls entered the dream (in hindsight, possibly as a form of protection). Afterward, I was transported by force to my mother's garden in Belfast while Cara stood by, looking peaceful and grinning widely. She asked Faye to guess her age, then laughed as Faye responded, 25. She wore a beautiful white dress and looked about four years old. Her friends, including Sarah-Jane and TC from high school, appeared in the garden afterward, seeming amazed about Cara's return to earth and how it related to Jesus rising from the dead. Sarah-Jane mentioned how she *"heard something about this before but didn't realise someone could come back to life."* The other kids were in awe. I observed TC staring at Cara in amazement and waking up thinking this was more than a dream.

6

FINN WITNESSES THE AFTERLIFE

'Why is there a pig's head floating around the bedroom'?

One morning as Finn dressed for school, he pointed to an orb floating around the room. He described how it moved slowly in a circular motion before disappearing. I didn't have my glasses handy and failed to spot it. I showed him a video of his third birthday party where Cara spoke movingly in her sweet little voice about his presents. She sat next to him on the floor, wearing the same grey school jumper. With her back turned in the video, he asked, "'Who is the girl in the grey school clothes"? He'll occasionally mention something about not remembering Cara but then tell us a tale about them both playing or getting up to mischief.

Maybe it's how a child deals with loss. Grief is a strange phenomenon. One minute we could laugh about Cara's antics and one-liners, and the next, we feel cut up. But we don't mope around or feel like the victims of great misfortune. We're 'grateful to God for small mercies' as my ma would say. We know many people with significant or advanced brain cancers, fighting desperately for survival against the odds as their families attempt to navigate through the chaos and complexity of the health system. An overwhelming sense of hopelessness tends to permeate due to the lack of innovations and limited funding for brain cancer. People are upset and seek a fair deal for their loved ones. It's unfathomable how Government spends so little money on brain tumours compared to other types of cancer. And disbelief because children and young people continue to use outdated chemotherapy treatments that are decades old and have serious side effects.

Finn woke in a panic early one March morning after experiencing a nightmare. An angry man in a garage shouted to him about the 'mark of the beast.' He looked dazed and confused and repeated the dream many times that day. We avoid mentioning that name and try to shield Finn from supernatural and paranormal activity. It was surreal that I'd vividly dreamt about Cara and my father that same night when 'Cara hugged her Granda, Paddy, at traffic lights'.

We often try to decipher the messages contained in these dreams. I remember, in a dream, visiting my father, Paddy, in a house on Mulholland Terrace in Belfast. He was in bed and not feeling well. I then went back and forth to St Paul's chapel. On another occasion, I awoke from a dream about yellow-coloured flowers and daisies in my grandparents Lily and Malachy's home to a slap in the back from Finn. He complained that my phone made a boxing ding noise that scared him at that moment. Neither Faye nor I heard a noise because I'd switched my phone off.

Shortly afterward, I felt the effects of the first Covid jab when a builder arrived to fit our new bath. He immediately switched the heating and water off. After experiencing shivery symptoms all day, I shared a few glasses of wine with Faye during the Champions League semi-final between Chelsea and Real Madrid. Later, I woke during the night with indigestion and struggled to drift back off.

Around 7 am, Finn's voice was barely audible behind me. After turning to face him, I noticed he was gazing and pointing to the picture in our bedroom.

He described seeing a 'face in the flowers, and a baby next to it.' I looked up and spotted medieval faces and one that resembled Padre Pio on the curtains immediately alongside it. We avoid discussing supernatural or paranormal activities around Finn as he's young. Still, I decided to ask Finn what he could see at the spot where Padre Pio's resemblance appeared, and he said, *"...it looks like a clown face with a hat".* So now the faces are revealing themselves to Finn.

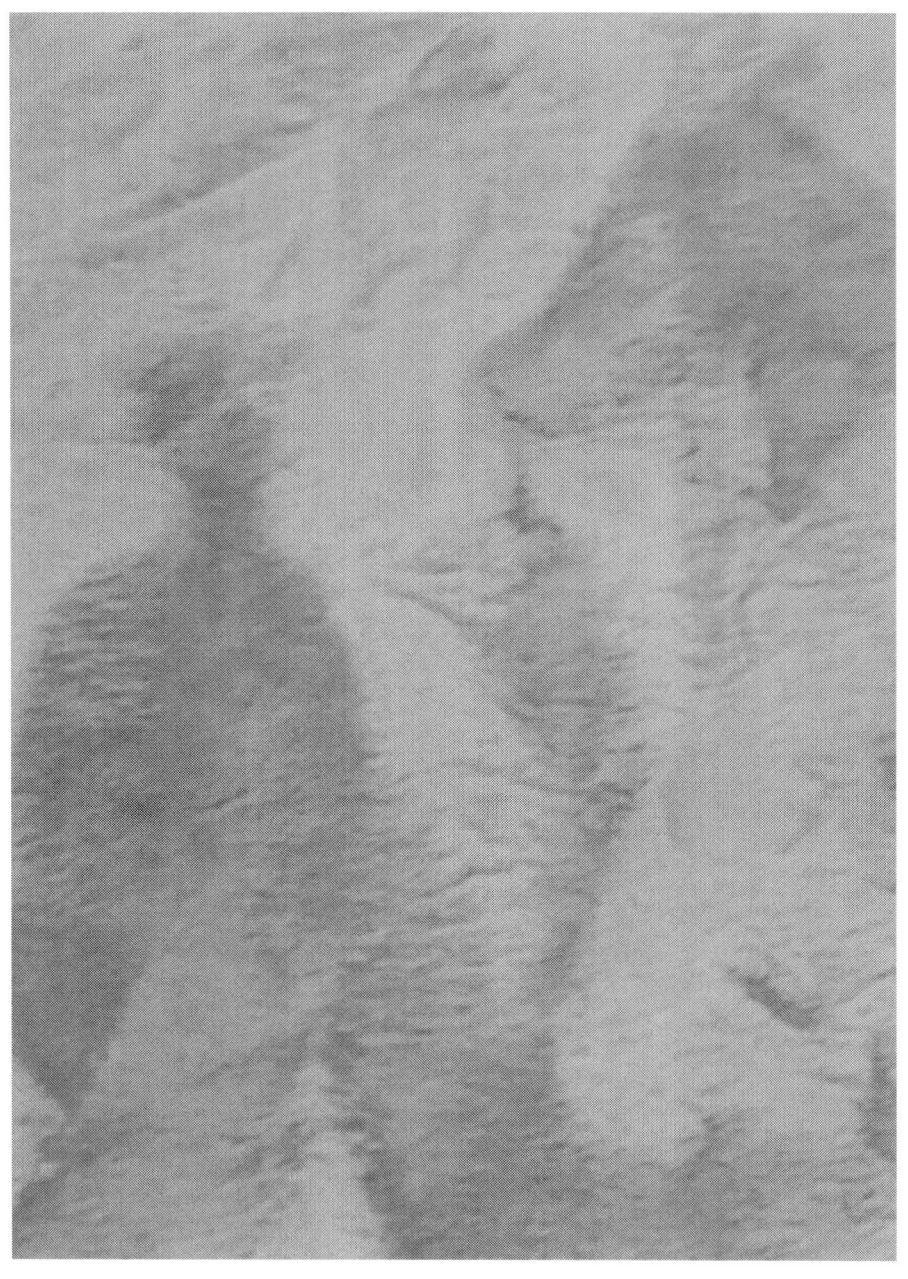

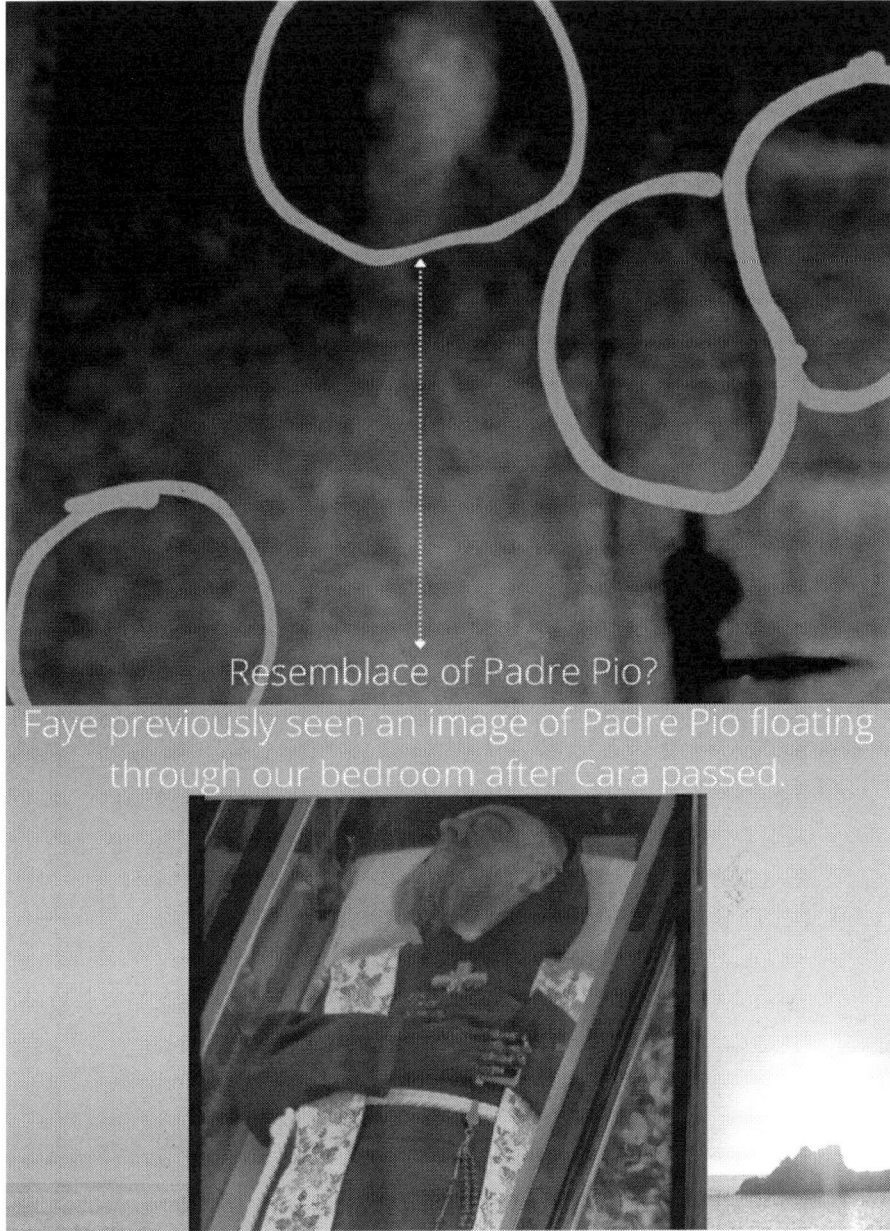

Fig. 7a Man and Horse; and Fig 7b. Padre Pio resemblance to picture of his body at rest. Sample of images that appear each day. The original images on @caramiamervyn Instagram site are more visible in colour.

While open to the spirit world, we sought Lorna Byrne's advice on how to deal with the activity. One cold September night, I had another vivid and surreal dream which seemed to last for ages. I sensed the dark side was close. I looked up (still dreaming), and he was staring me in the face, looking down from above my head, holding a pair of scissors as if ready to attack. It felt real and scary enough to wake me up, and I immediately prayed. Then after drifting off again, back in a dream, I was strolling through a housing estate with Faye. Suddenly, the same massive, sinister face appeared, peering at us from a large gable wall. I jumped up again and noticed that Finn and Faye were now awake.

On waking, Finn asked, "Daddy, why is there a pig's head floating around the bedroom."

How surreal. So, we scheduled another clearance (exorcism). We don't believe that it's the house itself. But we think the dark side is never far away from the site of prayers. We feel protected from Cara and other spiritual beings on the other side.

Fig. 8 Little girl appearing to pray, next to Finn

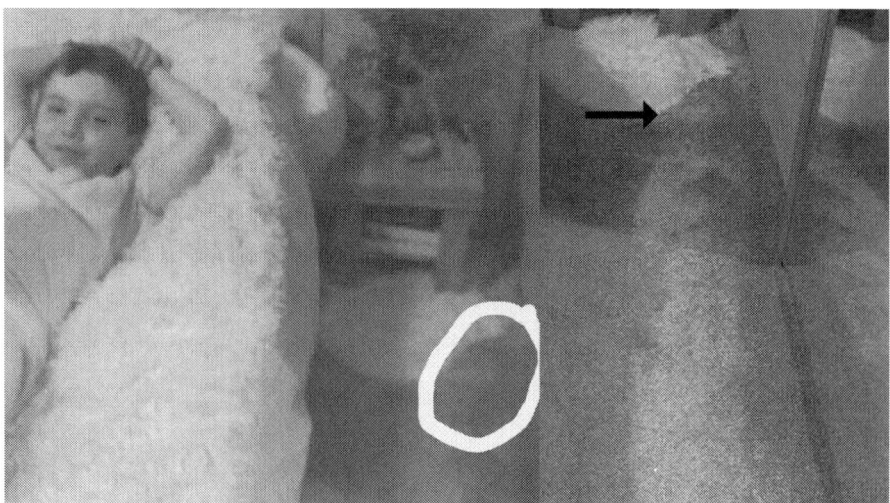

Bélmez Appearances in Spain 'La Casa de las Caras'

"María's home was advertised to the tourists as La Casa de las Caras (The House of the Faces)".

Our experiences resonate with some of the appearances in Bélmez, Spain which reportedly began on 23rd August 1971. A lady called María Gómez Cámara described what appeared to be a human face forming naturally through concrete on her kitchen floor.

Juan Pereira and Miguel (father and son) used a pickaxe to destroy the appearance before laying new concrete. However, images continued to form on the floor. This activity had political implications, and Bélmez's mayor intervened and forbade the new face from being desecrated or destroyed. The investigation team took several pictures for scientific study.

María's home generated a lot of inquisitive visitors and was subsequently renamed La Casa de las Caras (The House of the Faces). The Pereira family continued to report sightings of faces from both sexes and ages and with different expressions. In Burials and Beyond, 'The House of Faces' it was stated: But why did the faces appear?

In April of the following year, Professor De Argumosa travelled from Madrid to Bélmez after hearing about the case. He announced that, through his research, he had unearthed several historic documents reporting that a seventeenth-century governor of Granada (born in Bélmez) had murdered five members of a local family. The whereabouts of the murder site was vague but believed to have taken place nearby to or in the Pereira household itself.

Another theory posed by several sources was that, as the house was so close to a church, it was probably built on the site of an old cemetery. Indeed, when the floor was removed and fully excavated, human remains were found several feet below. Many of the skeletons had no skulls and the bodies were reinterred in a nearby Catholic cemetery. Some contemporary reports cite the excavated remains to have been dated around 700 years old.

It must be said that human remains were also found under other neighbouring houses. However, the Pereira house was the only one to report apparitions. After the removal of the remains and the replacement of the floor, the faces were expected to be a thing of the past. For a few weeks, this was the case, and the town resumed its day-to-day business. On 3rd February 2004, Maria Pereira passed away. Yet the faces continued to appear on her kitchen floor. In the supernatural, as in life, nothing is ever, ever simple. [ii]

As I prepared to submit the manuscript to Amazon for the pre-Christmas sale, I decided to search on Google Lens using a close-up picture of Figure 8. Guess what appeared in one of the images? A picture from the Bélmez Appearances in Spain.

Imagine the chances of Figure 8 from our home in Leeds having a direct connection to the images in Bélmez. And even spookier is the name 'La Casa de las Caras'.

7

DARK SIDE

"The angels have told me that Irish spirituality is different from others, which is one of the reasons why so many Irish people have chosen (or been forced by circumstances) to leave Ireland and intermarry in different parts of the world, mixing the unique Irish spirituality with other spiritualities" (Lorna Byrne).

THIS FIGURE APPEARED AS KIERAN, FAYE AND FINN DISCUSSED CARA AS THEY WALKED THROUGH COOKRIDGE, LEEDS.

NO OTHER LIGHTS SOURCES WERE EVIDENT.

Fig 9: Angel-like figure on our walk

We now understand that with light, orbs, and prayers, darkness is lurking. The Bible describes how the other side was once angels. Angels are merely light beings. They are not human but portray a human appearance for people on Earth. My family and friends believe that the orbs that we witness are angels. Lorna describes how angels get their light from God, and that's why they continually serve him. They are all connected to him - the good angels, and it's how they receive their light from him. However, the scriptures say that the other angels - Lucifer and his followers, became cut off from God when war broke out in Heaven, and God cast them out of Heaven. They were no longer connected to God and no longer receiving his light, so they were just beings opposite to light. They plug into the dark forces or energy of the universe rather than God's light because they desire power.

The Bible doesn't give us an exact timeline of Satan's origin. Rather, what we know of Satan's beginnings comes from passages written by the prophets Ezekiel and Isaiah, which Bible scholars believe detail the devil's fall from Heaven (Ezekiel 28; Isaiah 14). The prophets tell us that Satan was an angel known as the "morning star," translated as Lucifer (Ezekiel 28:14; Isaiah 14:12). As an angel, Lucifer walked on God's holy mountain and was anointed to serve God as a member of the guardian cherubim, among the highest rank of angels in God's holy host second only to the seraphim (Ezekiel 28:14).

That Lucifer has ordained a cherub was no small honour. In Heaven, the cherubim hold such a position of celestial prominence that God Himself sits "enthroned between the cherubim" (Isaiah 37:16). Lucifer's Pride Led God to Cast Him Out of Heaven. As believers, we know that Satan and his demons will ultimately be defeated and cast into the lake of fire for all eternity (Matthew 25:41). However, until the end times, Satan remains a powerful spiritual being whose sole aim is to deceive us into severing our relationship with God and with each other (John 8:44; Revelation 12:10).

My mother prays each day heavily and often recounts tales of harassment - especially during prayers. When she gave two elderly Belfast ladies a copy of our first book, *Is Mise Cara*, she heard some muttering from a loud, angry voice. After sleeping late one morning when fasting during Lent, she prayed before visiting the bathroom. On top of the landing, a sinister male voice uttered, 'Turn left, go downstairs and take that smirk off your face". Hinting, "stop fasting and go to the kitchen." My sister Carla has seen a smiling gorilla with large, crooked teeth when closing her eyes to pray, among many other experiences.

Lorna Byrne advised that although we can restrain the dark side, it won't completely leave. Prayers are critical for managing any negative situations that emerge. They often appear to spook spiritual people out. But we have been advised to show them strength, authority, and fearlessness. We demonstrate spiritual power by praying, frequent clearances, and using holy water. Lorna suggests that we are a billion times more powerful than any angel because we have a soul - that speck of light of God. That goes the same for the other side. We agree with Lorna that the more spiritual you are, the more you notice things around you and the world's beauty. Most people aren't awakened and disregard God's creation. It's because, as Lorna states, humanity has been blinded.

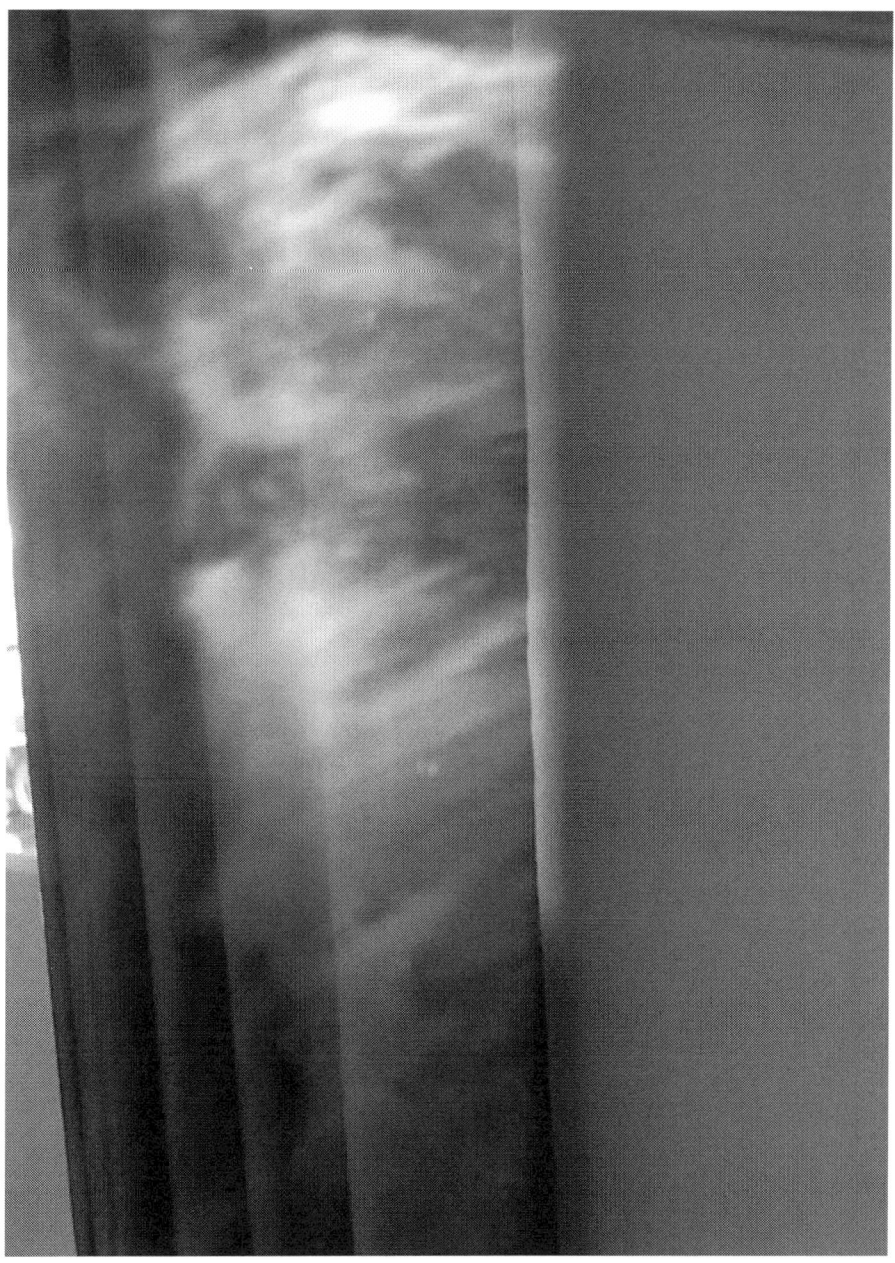

Figure 10. Type of figures floating around the home

We had a healthy scepticism of orbs, souls, and ghosts before Cara passed. We also dislike hearing or reading about other people's dreams. Still, we feel compelled to share some of our own unconscious experiences with real-time occurrences because they confound us. One morning, we discussed the death of another child via DIPG. His father then contacted me via WhatsApp minutes later. Again, it was the timing that surprised us. On the same day, I wrote a WhatsApp message to Pearl (Lorna Byrne's daughter and manager).

Kieran to Pearl: *"I'll send the book draft next week so you can check and approve Lorna's content. You were in my dream last night. You were with two other sisters. We were all in a pub. Everyone was in great form, laughing. Faye mentioned how you all changed your hair colour to blonde. But your hair looked light brown to me. I was telling you about my da, who isn't too well. Then one of your sisters started to talk about your [own] daddy (Joe). She was playfully copying his voice, saying something about the remote control and television in a strong Irish accent".*

In the previous chapter, we discuss how Orlaith mentioned for us to look out for a sign via the name Rose. In Chapter 5, we recalled messages from a different spiritual messenger called Rosie Walsh in May 2022. She mentioned Cara singing to my own da in his flat in Belfast. She laughed, recalling how he turned his remote control down to figure out where the noise was coming from.

"Ask him has he heard her singing lately around him? She shows me him muting the tv like he thought he heard something but wasn't sure, she says it was meeee!"

"She sends kisses to you all and shows me again the image of the group hug. The feeling of love is overwhelming; she truly is a special angel. I will keep you da in my prayers and hope all goes well. Was a pleasure".

Returning to my dream about Lorna's family. I remember being outside looking at the sky with my brother Damien. I could see lots of souls staring down. But the clouds looked dark. My brother mentioned sternly how a 'bad storm was on the way.' In another part of the dream, Lorna was in it. Then I was in a room with Faye and Finn, and the faces of wee souls were all over the room. I just thought I'd share that with you.

I know you only have one sister, Aideen, but it was a vivid dream. Like a running video, clear as day. Anyway! How random and mad? I said a wee prayer to Joe to look after you all. I hope Lorna is recovering well. Slan anois.

Pearl responded about the dream and mentioned how Lorna gradually improved from surgery. As Faye and I worked our way through draft pages of the current book, we were surprised to get to this text which we had written some months previously and forgotten about.

Lorna has previously explained how her soul left her body along with the soul of her unborn child. Upon arriving in Heaven, the angels informed her that she wasn't supposed to accompany the child. Occasionally, if someone experiences significant pain, their soul might leave the body. This perhaps explains why Lorna was shocked at the thought of being separated from her unborn child. She explains how her soul held on to the baby's soul and went to Heaven with the baby.

Fear (Faye Mervyn)

I wake up in the night with a breeze flowing by, I suddenly feel scared, but I know not to cry.

It's as if I have been watched, and "it" won't go away, but I know my Guardian Angel is guarding my way.

Not letting harm come on this day.

Figure 11. Little souls? Baby with hat to the left? Little faces to the right. See Instagram for clearer coloured pictures

8

JIM HOGAN FROM CORK

by Margaret O'Driscoll, Jim's mother

"Mom, you know I'm here so why do you let people make you feel that way? Tell people about our connection; we do live on spiritually"

Fig. 12 Jim Hogan

My son Jim was born on 19th August 1999. He weighed 8lb 9oz and was a beautiful, healthy baby. My mom (Jim's grandmother) cut his cord, and I called him Jim after my father. Jim is my second of three children: two boys and a girl. Stephen is my eldest, and Sasha the youngest. I loved being a mom and adored my kids.

When Jim was seven months old, he took ill. I brought him to the hospital, where he was diagnosed with pneumonia. He was put on an antibiotic drip and remained in the hospital for two weeks. I never left his side. Jim was always prone to chest infections, and when he was about two and a half years old, the doctors prescribed two inhalers for asthma. Jim remained sick and, at one time, had stints in the hospital twelve times a year.

At five years old, he had a serious asthma attack, and the doctors told me that I was fortunate to bring him when I did because he was extremely ill. Over time, Jim's asthma became more manageable as he aged. He came off the inhalers at ten years old, and his asthma seemed to have disappeared. I was so happy for Jim. He was a very kind, caring, and gentle boy with many friends. He had a great sense of humour, and his teachers at school would often praise him for his honesty and sense of humour. One of his teachers told me how Jim liked humming in class and when asked why he was humming, he said, "because he just wanted to."

Jim loved playing outside with his friends and enjoyed skateboarding. I would take Jim and his brother Stephen to the skateboarding park for hours. They enjoyed it and never wanted to leave. Jim also loved his food and the different flavours and spices. He relished almost everything that he ate and took his time. Always so calm; it would take him ages to prepare for school, short trips, and holidays. Seeing neighbours taking shopping from their cars, he would be straight out to help.

Jim was very close to his brother Stephen. They were best friends and always there for each other. When his sister Sasha was born, he was eight years old and happy to have a little sister. He loved holding and playing with her. He was also very good to me, would do anything I asked him, and when he was older, he would mind his sister while I was working. He started secondary school and excelled greatly. He loved playing the Xbox too. When he finished secondary school, he attended college for two years, became a personal trainer and nutritionist, and taught us all to eat healthier.

Jim graduated in 2019, and I was so proud of him. His tutor told me he was a pleasure to teach, a great guy, and a credit to me because he was just a respectable young man. He was the Best Man for his brother Stephen who got married in Lanzarote, and we had a great time on holiday afterward. Jim loved tattoos and had his first for his 16th birthday. I asked him what he would like for his birthday, and he said, "a tattoo." I was shocked but allowed him. After that, he wanted more and more tattoos. While working in a leisure centre doing personal training, they gradually increased. He ended up with two sleeves and more on his back.

Jim loved football, and he followed Liverpool football team. He would never miss a match. He was so happy when they won the league and danced around the kitchen. I have never seen him so happy. He loved visiting Liverpool, and in March 2020, he visited with his Fiancé and proposed to her on 14th February, St Valentine's Day. He was so romantic.

When returning from a weekend away, Jim had a seizure at Liverpool John Lennon Airport and was taken to hospital by ambulance. I rushed there from work when I got the call. Jim was kept in for a few days, diagnosed with epilepsy, and prescribed medication for his seizures. The doctors told Jim that he couldn't drive for six months. He was more upset about that than the seizure.

Being very disciplined, he quickly sold his car. Covid had just started, and the leisure centre had closed, but he didn't mind and got on with his life. That was Jim all over; nothing fazed him.

I came home from work one day, and Jim ran down the stairs, and he said, "Mom, I got accepted into the Irish Army." He was delighted, but I was shocked and didn't even know he had applied. But that was Jim; he was always full of surprises. One night, as we sat down to have dinner, he told me he had a fitness test due on 21st June. The plan was for me to drop him off before work and for his brother, Stephen, to collect him.

I dropped Jim at the Army Barracks and wished him the best of luck. I then phoned him on my lunch break, and he excitedly told me how he'd passed; he sounded delighted. When I returned from work, he told me about his plans to visit Limerick with the army at the end of September for three months of training. He knew by the look on my face that I was worried and said, "don't worry, mom - I'll be fine. I'll phone you every day, and sure it's only three months". I told him, "My children are my life and my whole world." I would mention that to them all the time.

But on 20th September 2020, my whole world was ripped apart. My daughter called out of the blue. She told me that Jim was already on the kitchen floor when she came downstairs and that she couldn't wake him. I told her to call our neighbours and phone an ambulance before driving home as fast as I could. I kept praying to God, "please let my son be okay." I knew when I entered the door and saw Jim that he was gone. I still did CPR in the hope that I was wrong. I'll never forget the agony, the pain in my heart, and the empty feeling inside of me. My life and my world were gone; my heart was broken.

My amazing, kind, caring, beautiful boy had departed, and I will never be able to live without one of my children. My worst fear in the world had come true. I asked my mother (his godmother) to mind him in Heaven for me. My mother went to Heaven in 2010, and I told my mother that I would be with them soon. After saying that in my head to my mother, I looked at Stephen and Sasha and thought, 'how could you put them through this pain'?

The next few days were the hardest of my life. I had to organise Jim's funeral and be there for my children. I don't know where I got the strength from. I think it was Jim, I do.

In honour of my son, we had a Liverpool-themed funeral. Everyone was to wear either a Liverpool jersey or simply red and white colours. He had a white casket and red pillow, and all his flowers were red and white. Our neighbours, friends, and family formed a guard of honour, and as Jim arrived at the church, we played his favourite song, "You'll Never Walk Alone." I stood on the altar and spoke about my son. I wanted everyone to know about my beautiful Jim. I then stayed at my son Stephen's house for a week. Stephen wanted me to stay with him longer, but I couldn't. I just kept feeling like I wanted to be close to Jim. I couldn't get him out of my head, so I told Stephen that I'd return home for the day to see how I'd feel. I just craved to return to the home of my son.

En route, I was nervous about how I'd feel, but when I opened the front door, I didn't have to worry because I immediately sensed my son and smelt his presence. I said, "I'm sorry I ran away, son; mom is home." I then felt at peace.

Later that night, I went to bed heartbroken, feeling so empty and wondering how I could carry on for the sake of my children. I'd not eaten or slept since my son woke up in Heaven. I went to bed and was devastated and crying when I suddenly felt something on my face. It was the sensation of being rubbed and a kiss on my forehead. I knew it was Jim and realised that no one and nothing could break my bond with my children.

Every night he would rub my face and kiss me. It had been about a month since Jim's transition behind the veil at that time, and I was barely eating and sleeping. Each time I tried to eat, I felt sick and also felt guilty about washing my face. I was lying in bed, devastated and crying when I suddenly felt Jim lying alongside me with his arms wrapped around me. I fell asleep and slept for a few hours.

I would frequently talk to Jim and tell him that I knew he was still with me. I wanted to see if he was happy, so I would say, "please, son, let me know you are happy." Then one night, just as I was falling asleep, Jim came to me and sat on my bed and said, "Mom, I'm happy, I am, and I'm okay. I'm sorry I had to leave you all, but I'm at peace".

We both sat on the bed for ages, and he said: "mom, I have to go now." I said I wanted to go with him, but he said, "You can't, mom. Sasha and Stephen need you".

I remember thinking that if I went with Jim, Sasha would find me in the morning. I was even looking at myself lying in bed, and Jim's arms were still around me. He said, "you have to go back," but I didn't want to. I kept thinking, 'Stephen won't believe that I found Jim", and then it was as if someone had given me an electric shock. I bounced up off the bed and was feeling ill the next day. My chest was sore, and I kept thinking about what had happened during the night. I knew then that we would never die; we just shed our human bodies.

Every night since Jim went to Heaven, he kisses me goodnight and rubs my face. As a family, my kids would kiss me goodnight, and we would always say, "goodnight, I love you. I'll see you in the morning". So, I have continued to do that, and I still kiss Jim's photo on my fireplace and say goodnight and good morning to him.

I asked Jim for signs, and when I got up that morning, three white feathers were on my kitchen floor. I've found white feathers all over my house. In the sitting room, the hall, my stairs, and my bedroom. I had three butterflies in my home—one in my room, one in the bathroom, and one in my kitchen.

One night I was getting into bed, and as I pulled back the bed covers, I noticed a white feather on my bed. I called my daughter and showed her, and she said, "mom, that's Jim; he's letting us know he's with us."

Since the transition, my son has told me that the white feathers are to know that he's still here. I now keep a large jar of white feathers on my fireplace. I have pots in my sitting room and bedroom, and wherever I find the feathers, I leave them in that room.

Sasha feels Jim's presence, too. He sits on her bed some nights, and she has felt his arms around her too. My son Stephen and his wife and children also told us how they feel his presence. My grandkids remarked, "Nana, Jim lives in our house and up in the sky. And he plays with us in our room".

I know my son Jim is still with us all. He has just shed his human body and is with us spiritually. I know now that nothing and no one can break the bond that we have with our loved ones and especially our children, and nothing could break the bond between a mother, brothers, and sisters.

I was sitting in my kitchen one morning after my daughter had gone to school when I heard the word "Mom"; it was Jim's voice. I said, "I know you're here, son." Jim gets annoyed with me when I don't share the connection. Sometimes, when I'm hesitant, he says, "Mom, you know I'm here. So why do you let people make you feel that way? Tell people about our connection; we live on spiritually".

So now, whenever someone enquires about my son and how I am keeping, I tell them, "My son is still with me. I just don't see him physically". Jim is very happy when I do that. He has told me he's living his best life, is happy, and travels wherever. There is no time in Heaven, and he's with my mother, his cousins, and loved ones.

Another time he said, you "would love it up here; it's all shiny and so bright," and how he forgives anyone that hurt him and how he lives in pure love. I meditate every morning, and my bond with my son is getting stronger and stronger, putting my heart at peace. Jim comes to me while I meditate and even takes me to Heaven, but he doesn't like it when I don't want to return.

We had a Liverpool headstone made especially for Jim. The gates of Heaven are etched on his gravestone, which says: "You'll Never Walk Alone," Now I know that is so true. I never thought I could get over one of my children going to Heaven and leaving me. Still, my son Jim ensures that we will never be apart, and I'm so grateful to him for that. He knew I could never live without him, so he confirmed I didn't have to. He keeps sending me so many signs.

After writing this chapter, I went out to my front garden because it was a lovely sunny day for tea. When I sat on the bench, I looked down, and there was a beautiful white feather by my feet. I looked to Heaven and said: "Thank you, my son. I love you so much".

Kieran and Faye

We now continue with Margaret's story about her son Jim Hogan and illustrate similarities with our experience after losing Cara. In the next chapter, Margaret discusses how she was contacted by Lorna Byrne with a message from her son Jim, helping her through the dark times. Reading about Margaret's experience was akin to reading about ourselves and Cara in an incredible example of what appears to be more meaningful synchronicities.

9

A MIRACLE FROM HEAVEN

by Margaret O'Driscoll, Jim's mother (continued)

Words can't describe how much Lorna helped me and my family escape a very dark place. I truly believe Lorna is God's daughter walking among us like his son Jesus walked among us too.

A few weeks after my son Jim went to Heaven, I was tidying my bedroom and came across a box of angel books that I hadn't seen in years and started to read them. I then told a friend, Eileen, about how I came across them. She then asked which one I was reading, and I replied, "Angels in my Hair," and explained how I'd had the book for a long time. One week later, Eileen called again, and we continued to discuss the book. She then asked if she could see it. After showing it to her, she looked at me and said, "Is this the right book? This is 'Guided by Angels', not 'Angels in my Hair". I was shocked to hear that, convinced it was the latter. Eileen suggested, "this may be a sign from your angels telling you to get the book."

The next day, when visiting Ballincollig with my daughter, I asked her to Google and see if a book exists called 'Angels in my Hair. Sure enough, there was. Lorna Byrne was the author. I immediately entered Eason's bookshop and bought it. Later that night, I began to read the book. I couldn't sleep much since Jim went to Heaven and hadn't slept properly for about three weeks. Reading Lorna's book that night saved me from a dark place. It brought peace into my head and hope that Jim's Guardian Angel was with him while he went to Heaven.

The following day I asked my daughter to download Instagram for me so I could send Lorna a message. I wanted to tell her about my son Jim and my family. How his death ripped our world and hearts, and how devastated we all were. I was surprised to receive a reply from Lorna. I just wanted to let someone know how I was feeling. A few days passed, and I wasn't expecting a response. But to my surprise, when I checked online, I noticed that Lorna had seen my message and asked her daughter Pearl to reply and tell me that Lorna requested a Skype call. I couldn't believe it! I was delighted. All I wanted to know was that my son was okay. I kept asking him since he went to Heaven.

Lorna Byrne Skyped me on 20th January 2021 and had a message from Jim. She said:

> **"Jim asked God for a miracle. It was for God to find a way for me to find and contact Lorna so Jim could tell me he was okay; and that he was with his Nana (my mother and Jim's godmother) and my brother Patrick."**

Lorna told me that Jim was not alone and that his Guardian Angel took his soul straight to Heaven. Jim didn't suffer any pain and was in Heaven before he fell onto the floor. Jim also said that he was with me, Stephen, and Sasha all the time and that he wasn't gone. He said,

> *"The day I woke up in Heaven, I sat outside Sasha's bedroom door to stop her from going downstairs for as long as possible so that you'd have time to return home from work".*

I will be forever grateful for Lorna. After that video call, I started thinking, "you know what? I will get through this - for Jim, Stephen, Sasha, and my grandchildren".

Lorna would Skype me every few weeks and invite me, my children, grandchildren, and Stephen's wife, Michaela, down to her home. Lorna said that Jim wanted us all to come to her home for the day. We visited on 1st August 2021 and had lunch with Lorna, Pearl, and Pearl's children. We had the most amazing day with Lorna and her family. We'd had a beautiful lunch after going to the sanctuary and picking some fresh vegetables. The sanctuary must be the most amazing place I have ever visited. Lorna gave us all one-on-one time and spoke privately to us about Jim and the messages he had for us. Lorna told us that Jim never gives up, and when he wants something, he pesters her and God and loves us all so much.

Lorna also told me that we are a "gene of pure love as a family" and that it was "very rare." We felt amazing relief when we came home from spending the day with Lorna and her family. Simply knowing Jim was happy, at peace, and not alone was precious. He was now with all the family that went before him.

Lorna gave us all the most amazing blessings. We almost felt an electric current running through our bodies as she prayed over us. She healed a lot of our pain that day. Lorna is still in contact with our family. She gave me free tickets for a spiritual healing event at her sanctuary. There were 50 of us in attendance; it was the most beautiful day.

Words can't describe how much Lorna helped me and my family escape a very dark place. I truly believe Lorna is God's daughter walking among us like his son Jesus walked among us too.

Kieran and Faye

Throughout this journey, we sought alternative perspectives from people with different experiences, e.g., experiencing loss or perhaps going through difficult circumstances. The next story takes an independent journalist's mindset to provide a wider interpretation of meaningful synchronicity.

10

ALENA STEWART (SLOVAKIA)

by Alena Stewart on Synchronicity

I am honoured to tell you about synchronicity from my perspective. I'm a Slovak woman living in Ireland who lost her parents to cancer as a teenager, so I know the heartache of losing someone dear. Later in my life, I started writing for a Slovak spiritual magazine. My first article from April 2021 was about synchronicity! It contained many amazing real-life stories I collected from friends and strangers. Then I read *'Is Mise Cara: Orbs, Souls and Holy Ghosts'* and was so touched and fascinated by the story that I asked to interview Kieran and Faye. I'm very grateful that they agreed. The magazine published the article in the July 2021 issue.

In the same issue, another author (whom I didn't know) wrote about resilience. They also quoted the ancient fable of a Chinese farmer and his son that Father Emmanuel had read at Cara's funeral! If you don't know how it goes:

A Chinese farmer gets a horse, which soon runs away. A neighbour says, "That's bad news". The farmer replies, "Good news, bad news, who can say?". The horse comes back and brings another horse with him. Good news? The son rides the second horse, falls, and breaks his leg. Bad news? The

ALENA STEWART (SLOVAKIA)

Emperor's men come to take all healthy young men to fight in a war. They spare the farmer's son.

To see this story in the same magazine, just a few pages away from Cara's piece – was it synchronicity or a coincidence? I'm still not sure. The same story reappeared in the same magazine a few months later.

Some people say that there are no coincidences. I'm too left-brained to go as far as that. But some coincidences are so big, weird and magical that one needs to wonder. Here is one which happened to me and made me feel better during a difficult period. It also made me feel special - as if the Universe cared for my trials.

My long-term Irish boyfriend, studying abroad, suddenly started talking about breaking up. It was very hard for me; I didn't want it to happen. And just at that time, a wreath with my boyfriend's first name Glen appeared on the bridge over the canal near my house in Dublin, which I passed every day! I know someone with the same name must have died there. Still, it was also a personal confirmation that our relationship was ending.

Many synchronicities involve a thing or person you've just been pondering. In my case, the wreath appeared as a symbol of the dying relationship with my boyfriend. Before a breakup, girls and women often mention the loss or breaking of a necklace, heart-shaped stone, or key chain (from the boyfriend or even with his photo). These are all symbolic means to signal a major change.

It's also very common to think of a person and then be surprised to see them or receive an unexpected call from them. An acquaintance who works as a therapist said that a patient she hasn't seen for a year or so often comes to her mind, and they get back in contact the next day. She doesn't even find it surprising anymore because it always happens. Here are some other examples from my friends:

"I used to have a crush on a boy with the surname Straka (which translates as 'Magpie'). One day during a car journey, I remembered him, which made me think about the birds. I told my Mam, who was with me, that I hadn't seen magpies for a long time. I looked up, and they were, sitting on the electric cables like swallows! I'd never seen them like that before".

"Once I was on a bus and suddenly started thinking of someone I hadn't seen in years, and she was waiting at the next bus stop!"

"A few days ago, I was driving to work. For some reason, I remembered my old primary school teacher, wondering if she was alive, survived the pandemic, etc. I had not seen her for years. When I arrived at the City Council, where I work, I found her standing at the reception!"

Synchronicity can come in other forms too. The following are two examples from Slovak acquaintances that they experienced in forest settings and came as pleasant surprises to them.

"I went for a weekend walk with my family and had some dark thoughts. I split from my family and strolled down a different path – I'll go up to that tree, one more tree, two more. There was a beautiful silence there, it was snowing gently, and I felt peace in my soul and then I said: this will be the last tree, and I'll go back to my family. And on that last tree, a big angel was engraved into the bark. I felt everything would be good again".

I will now share another experience that happened to me 20 years ago. We were walking on the path through the forest, and I noticed a tree with a tiny hole in it. I went to it, put my hand in the spot, and there was a sweet chocolate inside, wrapped. I ate it! It was a moment of connecting to thoughts, (global) consciousness, telepathy, and whatever we don't know how to use. Or we knew but have forgotten".

I think synchronicities are those events when you think, "What are the odds?" And they seem so magical and out of this world that you lose your normal critical thinking and submerge in the moment. The girl from the last story wouldn't normally relish a piece of chocolate left by who-knows-who and who-knows-when. Also, as Robert Hopcke, a psychotherapist and an author of several books commented:

> "In all synchronicities, what is important is not the 'objective facts of the coincidences but the emotional impact they had on the people involved".

My Irish husband also remembers a few events that made him shake his head and be in awe:

> In my mid-thirties, I lived alone in a small town, far from my friends and felt lonely. I was also unhappy with my job and decided to change it and move back to a city where I had lived before and find some like-minded housemates. After I moved, I rented a room in temporary accommodation and set out to find a new home with new friends. My first stop was a vegetarian café that hosted a famous notice board of events, therapies, and accommodation opportunities.

> I had prepared a poster and found a space to put it up. After pinning it to the wall, an old acquaintance (who I hadn't seen for years and didn't even know was living in this city) emerged from the café. "Oh, you live here?" he asked me. I told him I was hoping to, and he said he had two friends looking for a housemate. I met them, we clicked, and I made two new lifelong friends after I moved in.

> I volunteered to tell a story about Pinocchio to a group of children. I was spending a week at an alternative festival in England and thought

this would be fun. However, I realised I only knew the little story of Pinocchio apart from the behaviour of his infamous nose. I would need to find out, but first, I needed to secure some props. I thought to myself: if I had the centre from a couple of empty rolls of kitchen towels, I could join them together and make a 'sliding nose' that would grow with each lie.

Then a thought occurred to me: have a look in the bins at the kitchen tents. I went, and sure enough, two empty rolls were sitting at the top of two recycling bins. Next, to find out the story. That day, and the next, I asked everyone if they could enlighten me; however, no one knew. However, I didn't forget the gap in my knowledge and continued to ask around. On my way to a shop on the final morning, I asked if anyone needed anything. One guy I hadn't met before was reading the morning paper in his van. A brand-new hardback copy of Pinocchio was sitting face up in front of him and within my reach. "You can have it", he told me. It had come free in that morning's paper.

Lots of these synchronicities happen when you need them most—for instance, giving comfort during a breakup or cheering up a depressed friend. Trish and Rob MacGregor refer to 'trickster synchronicities' in their book 'The 7 Secrets of Synchronicity'. A good example is the Pinocchio book which was found too late to be useful because the children had left the camp. Yet it served as a reminder of a deeper layer to our existence.

Kieran and Faye

A random selection of events made us think that the spirit world is even closer than we think. My brother Damien, his wife Jacqui and son Emmet visited a remote inlet in rural Ireland on a wet and windy day. He mentioned how there "wasn't a sinner about", an old Irish saying, for the place was empty and quiet. He prayed at a statue of Our Lady before attempting to light a candle. Each of his lighters wouldn't work, and a frail old lady strolled past as he was about to leave. Asking if she had a light, the old lady offered him a box of matches before wandering off. After lighting the candle, he saw the matchbox named 'CARA'.

In another example, Faye and I enjoyed a Saturday evening meal in Leeds. After asking the waiter to recommend a bottle of wine, he remarked that he "knew a good one". We discussed Cara when the waiter arrived with a bottle of wine with the label 'CaraCara'.

Alena Stewart Continued

I kept a few more powerful stories for the end of this chapter from two British women in my meditation group. Their contributions reflect the quote by psychotherapist Deike Begg in 'Synchronicity: The Promise of Coincidence':

"The most interesting aspect of all truly synchronistic phenomena is that there appears to be a pre-existing knowledge of things to come, things of which we have at that moment no apparent awareness whatsoever. There seems to be an altogether 'other' that knows more than us, can see into the future and also has the creative ability to find the quickest route to return us to our destined path."

Train Accident: Mind the Gap

My friend and workmate aged 20 and I (then aged 25) were involved in an underground train accident. Unfortunately, he didn't survive, and I have had major health issues.

About a year after the accident, I went on a retreat while still on crutches. It was my first big leap into the world of Spirit and Spirituality. A couple of massive synchronistic events occurred on the trip and just after.

One was that the woman I connected with who gave me a lot of healing dreamt that her phone was ringing the night before we met. Eventually, when she picked it up, the voice said: "Please mind the gap" (this is a repeated message in London underground stations). When she told me this, we were with her partner, and he was listening to music and looked freaked out because the song lyrics said the same thing at the same moment (the lyrics went "mind the gap, mind the girl").

Oracle Cards

The other story happened on the same retreat. I'd never used oracle cards before. I thought it was all a bit crazy and just had the confidence to use them because everyone was asleep in the place we were sharing, and I had woken up early. So, I read the instructions in the book. Since, at that time, I was in a tricky place with my boyfriend, I asked for guidance on a relationship. And as I was shuffling, a card flew out of the deck onto the floor. I was shocked – the card was of Jesus, and it said: "Open your heart to love". Then I read the description in the book, and it resonated so much that I had tears falling down my eyes and knew what the guidance was saying.

When I went home, I ordered the pack straight away. When it arrived, I opened it, and the first card was the same Jesus card I had got, but not only that, there were two identical Jesus cards. If you use oracle cards, you know you never get duplicates!

The message I got from that card was profound; the boyfriend is now my husband. Another significant layer of this is that I was born on Christmas Day. My name emanates from Mary, so I have always felt close to the figure of Jesus.

Fig. 13 The duplicate taro received in the pack

The Phone Box

Recently, during the COVID-19 lockdown, I was in quite a depressed state: I was breastfeeding my baby, I had just relocated back to the UK, and I was in a bad space. I asked for some spiritual guidance and wanted a sign. I agreed with God or the Universe that my sign would be an old-fashioned British phone box you don't see very often nowadays. I went on a day trip later that day with my family. I was walking down the street, and one was in front of me. As I walked towards the phone box, I kept repeating: "Surely it can't be that simple. It's too straightforward, too simple." I went to the phone box, and there was a sign on it. On an A4 piece of printed paper was the phrase: *What were you expecting?* And it just felt like that message on the phone box was for me.

Lost and Found

Last year when I was in Spain, I left all my five rings in the hotel room, all belonging to my Mam, who had died a few years before. They were all sentimental value – rings she had since she was a child and her engagement ring, which we used when I got engaged to my husband. The hotel insisted they were not there. I called several times again and explained where I had left them. "No, no, not there" was always the answer.

I set myself a clear intention that I would not let the rings go, that they were coming back to me. Then seven or eight weeks passed. I woke up in the morning on the anniversary of my Mam's death to an email from the hotel saying that they couldn't believe it, they went to clean the room that day, and all the rings were there. I don't know what happened; the fact that it happened on the day of my Mam's anniversary, it's miraculous.

Synchronicities are sometimes hard to distinguish from other phenomena. These include telepathy, foresight, manifestation/visualisation and pre-birth soul contracts. People take different routes, such as tapping into their collective mind/consciousness and getting help from spirit guides, angels or loved ones on the other side. But that's ok.

Although I would like to have everything nicely squared away in boxes, it may not be possible in this life.

As Trish and Rob MacGregor[ii] explain:

"Synchronicity is the Granddaddy of all paranormal phenomena, telepathy, precognition, clairvoyance, and remote viewing".

So, everything is interconnected and part of the higher realms. And I hope we will all continue to experience these wonderful moments and never forget that life is not just what meets the eye.

Kieran and Faye

Sceptics would often say that feathers stem from birds. Lorna Byrne acknowledges such an objective reality. However, she affirms that their appearance's emotional significance and timing count. They seem to land at moments when we need a helping hand.

On one occasion, a white feather floated into Faye's hand as we walked through Headingley in Leeds while talking about the structure of our new charity.

The Feather (Faye Mervyn)

I find a white feather; it gives me such joy.
It floats from the sky and lands on my door.
I smile to myself as I know that it's you; you have sent me a message showing me all that is true.
The feather is pure and brightens my day,
As if Heaven is showing me that we will meet again someday.

Another incident from several years ago concerned our friends in Belfast. Before Cara was born, they sent a bouquet after hearing of Faye's first miscarriage. We returned to the kitchen to find the flowers had fallen and lay scattered over the kitchen floor. There was no explanation for how they fell. Later that day, we received the news that our friend's younger brother had passed away unexpectedly.

In other sections of this book, including the chapter on Cara's 14th birthday in Heaven, we discuss other incidences of white feathers appearing in unusual places. Our friends agreed on the spiritual interconnection between all of this.

On the night of Cara's death, my brother Damien described significant signs, which now appear to be a warning in advance. In the chapter 'Message from Uncle Damien' he talks of black feathers as an omen:

"Black pillows adorned the sofa. Black feathers on the pillows were discarded and fell to the floor.
They reminded me of death, darkness and an old Irish film called Darby O'Gill and the Little People.
In the film, a funeral director brought a black funeral horse to remove a body from a home. Black feathers decorated the horse's face.

I visited the bathroom, and as the light shone upon the curtains, it resembled a black funeral veil.
I told Jacqui how this place made me feel uneasy before we left for Nancy's Bar.
Jacqui remarked how she was texting Faye and how Cara had a slight temperature but would be keeping an eye on her." [iv]

11

SIGNS FROM NIGERIA

"For starters, it means there is an important message from Cara. Usually, it will be associated with an Omen".

b y Benjamin Samuels

On 29th November 2020, I talked with a friend called Victor Thompson. Little did I know that this was a meaningful synchronicity linked with someone we both know. Thus, it was more than multiple coincidences. In that same year, in December 2020, Kieran spoke to me about printing a thousand copies of *Is Mise Cara*. They lost Cara on 29th December 2019 and witnessed surreal activities in their home and all around them afterward

It was touching and highly emotional to learn of the passing on of his beautiful daughter. I wondered how he and his family would be feeling. Kieran had helped me fight adversity (after losing my ex-wife) that almost consumed me; how could this be happening to him? I thought to myself. Around that time, my newly wedded wife and I were expecting our second child together. The consultant had given the expected delivery date between 20th December 2020 and the 1st week of January 2021. I remember asking Kieran if we could name our child after Cara. That seemed like the most honourable thing to do, given the man's impact on my life.

We previously discussed the faith healer Orlaith's question about the significance of December 20th.

Fig 14 Benjamin's parents in Nigeria

In the *Is Mise Cara* chapter' Sense-Making/Seeking Alternative Perspectives', Benjamin Samuel discussed his experiences and perceptions of the afterlife.

"For starters, it means there is an important message from Cara. Usually, it will be associated with an Omen. After my dad died, he'd often visit my mum in her dream, with his wedding suit and all that. He'd be asking her to come with him. She often confessed that to me. I always encouraged her against it, though.

Finally, she followed him after five years; she was buried in her wedding gown. You might not find this interesting, but that's how we interpret this; seeing the dead, even in dreams, is a worry for us. It is usually backed up with intensive and aggressive prayers..." (p.207)

You see, Cara had passed-on on 29th December 2019. My wife and I married on 29th December 2018. We were soon expecting a child and the expected delivery date was our anniversary (29th December 2020). My dad passed on 29th December 1998, and my wife had also been through a very trying moment on 29th December, many years before we met. She had lost someone very dear, someone, she'd been married to for only six months.

Something was striking about the number 29. Cara was born at 29 weeks. She had such a beautiful name, and such a lovely personality, even though we never had the opportunity of meeting her in person. My wife gave birth on 2nd January 2021, just after the new year.

We named our baby boy Cara (translated as 'God Saves Everything My Friend' or 'My Beloved'). 'God saves everything' is the meaning of Hakiz-Imana, and 'My Friend or My Beloved' is the meaning of Cara. Just a way of telling Kieran how close we felt to Cara.

Let's return to the printing of the book in Nigeria. Until I wrote these words, I had no idea why Dr Kieran and his wife Faye chose me to print the book on their daughter in Nigeria. There were a lot of his students in Africa before me. He had lots of friends in Nigeria, and he had high-profile friends that knew high-profile people in Nigeria, but he chose me.

Fig. 15 Incredible support from all faiths in Nigeria for our first book, Is Mise Cara

It has nothing to do with naming our child after Cara because we had this conversation about printing the books even before then. Whatever informed their decision remains an attribute of these multiple meaningful synchronicities.

On 8th February 2021, Kieran and Khalid transferred money to my bank account to print 1,000 copies of *Is Mise Cara* in Nigeria. Khalid Mukhtar is one of the people that Cara visited after she passed. He always reminds me of Pakistani Prime Minister Imran Khan; they have a striking resemblance.

Well, Kieran sent in the USD denomination earlier, so the need for conversion into Nigerian Naira came into play. At that time, there were exchange rate discrepancies in Nigeria, so I struggled with getting my contacts in Lafia, Nasarawa State, to convert this money. As stated above, I remembered my conversation with Victor Thompson. I decided to check in with the one person I could count on in this regard - Victor Thompson.

We met with Victor Thompson in our online class discussion forum during our first module, Leading and Learning in a Dynamic Era, in 2015. Kieran officiated this module from 2012 to 2021. Of all the people I know who could have converted money from USD to NGN denominations for printing copies of the book, Victor was the chosen one. Quite remarkable considering that Nigeria has a population of approx. 210 million. Six plus hours away from me via road transport in Lagos. One phone call, bank deposits, and WhatsApp chats took care of the first $US1,000 that served as part payment for the commencement of printing of *Is Mise Cara* copies in Nigeria.

These multiple synchronicities are very interesting and meaningful enough to summarise what transpired as we worked towards printing copies of *Is Mise Cara* in Nigeria. There is a powerful message in all that has played out and all that is playing out. I pray that God will give Kieran, his wife, and their entire family the wisdom to discern the messages in these synchronicities.

As for my entire family and me, these synchronicities speak to us in boundless measures. Especially the need to tune our minds into spreading a powerful message - a message of healing, a message of the existence of the afterlife.

Kieran and Faye

Ben's experiences remind us of other connections to the number 29. Cara was born at 29 weeks gestation and died on 29th December 2019, and our wedding anniversary date is 29th July. Cara's expected delivery date was due on 30th April 2008, and her brother Finn was born on 30th April 2015. In the chapter 'The God Spot' in *Is Mise Cara,* we wrote:

'Finn turned five years old on 30th April 2020, and it was his first birthday without Cara. I passed my driving test on 30th April 2008, which was also Cara's initial due date".

Raheema and the Car Crash

In another twist of fate which makes us think that dreams merge with reality, we share my dream of Ben's daughter, which coincided with a real-life serious car accident.

One night, I dreamt that Benjamin (Ben) Samuel's daughter Raheema was in our home in Leeds. Holding her hand, I walked her to a picture of Cara and asked, "Who is that?". Raheema replied in an excited voice, "That's Cara". The next day, I relayed my dream to Ben in Nigeria. He immediately responded about a car accident and believed that Cara's intervention saved them from serious harm.

Ben Samuel: Wow, tell you, Dr Kieran, in Abuja on Tuesday, we were supposed to go to ShopRite (a mall) with my colleagues. I wanted to buy Raheema's birthday bike. They all refused and insisted we should go the next day on Wednesday. I refused and went alone on Tuesday. The next Wednesday, my Raheema's Proprietress called to tell me that she and my wife were taking Raheema to the hospital. Raheema was shouting badly, screaming, saying [it's] her stomach. So, I told them at the seminar, and they permitted me to leave for my child's health.

[After the seminar] my colleagues [then] had a terrible car accident. All were lucky to be alive and shaken up, with two of them badly injured. Tell me something, Sir?

Kieran: Someone somewhere was protecting you and Raheema. And for Raheema to be in my dream, talking to Cara's picture. We'll pray for their speedy recovery. God works in mysterious ways. How is Raheema now? These messages are so powerful.

Ben Samuel: That's why I am telling you this, else I never would have mentioned it. I was protected from being in that car... I'd have 'been', put [seriously injured or killed].

As this is a book of hope, it is important to show that synchronicities occur in other contexts. On a much lighter note, the following section discusses an infamous series of true events that occurred in West Belfast between the 1970s and 1990s.

Falls Road Knockdowns

Not wanting to distract from the core premise of our book, I was hesitant to share these 'knockdown' stories with a wider audience. However, it is important to show that meaningful synchronicities know no bounds. So,

I'll now share a bizarre series of occurrences that happened to our family on a short (1/4 mile) stretch of road in West Belfast. Cara often found these stories amusing and bemusing.

Cara would often gasp when I told her about her Granda Paddy's car accident in the 1970s. He was trailed for several meters and found badly injured outside the Royal Victoria Hospital. Shortly afterward, he suffered serious injuries when a milk float machine crashed into his hands at Kennedy's Milk Factory in Belfast. He has been disabled ever since.

Once his legs started to give way, he purchased a new mobility scooter. My mum was on an Ulster bus from town on a cold winter night and wondered why a tiny light whizzed past the window. She looked again, and the flash passed her a second time. She then noticed that it was Paddy on his new mobility scooter, smoking what we refer to as a cigarette the size of a small snooker cue.

More knockdowns occurred. I was hit by a car outside the old Heinzes Pub on the Falls Road when five years old and experienced some scratches and bruises but nothing serious. After we moved house to Beechmount, our dog Shane was knocked down and killed outside the old Ulster Bank in Beechmount on the Falls Road. We buried Shane in the old Riddles Field (the site of Our Lady's Hospital) next to Beechmount Leisure Centre. As kids, we often heard tales of a ghost called 'Jimmy Riddle' who supposedly haunted the old leisure centre and nearby old folk's home.

Shortly afterward, my sister Lisa was seriously injured in a car accident and spent many months in recovery. Then I was hit by a car a few years later while crossing at the same spot from the opposite side. All knocked down on the same ¼-mile stretch of road. Our dog Prince must have sensed the danger. He'd often wait at the zebra crossing for other people to cross before following them—the only sensible one. Cara often wondered aloud if we were a 'few slices short of a loaf' such was her quirky sense of humour.

Cara's Love of Animals

Cara frequently asked us to share stories from our childhood. For instance, Cara wasn't allowed a pet because of her breathing problems. She loved all animals, and Faye often called her a wee 'mother hen' when around any animal.

We had lots of mad stories to tell from life in Belfast. How her aunt Lisa studied at Sunderland University and smuggled a living rabbit under her arm on a flight from Newcastle to Ireland. The poor thing only lasted a few days before Cara's cousin Kirsty fed it a dry cornflake and choked to death. Poor Cara didn't know whether to laugh or cry when we told her about Nana's joke about the 'cereal killer.

We bought Cara a goldfish when living in Bramley. She was only a child but became fascinated, watching in awe as it spun around aimlessly on its travels. There were tears before bed as we buried it in tin foil in the back garden after it passed. The next morning, there was the surreal sight of a beautiful magpie lying dead next to a clump of tin foil. It smelt the fish, plucked it from the soil, ate it and choked to death next to the cluster of disturbed ground.

We share stories of feathers appearing in the most bizarre places, especially when speaking about Cara. Resemblances of animals occasionally appear on walls and floors alongside human souls when we mention her name. Squirrels or birds are often visible when we pray in her bedroom. As I typed these words in my office, I heard Finn telling Faye about a robin that appeared at the window.

We once filmed a squirrel chasing orbs outside Cara's room. On another occasion, we captured a large bird at the window. It stared in and fluttered its wings when praying to Cara. At another time, as Faye texted a lady called Charlene in Craigavon, a beautiful cat with grey piercing eyes appeared and stared in the window next to Cara's seat.

Mise Éire

One evening in February 2021, I witnessed a range of faces around the home – many of which were difficult to decipher. So, I prayed to my Guardian Angel and, in particular, the Archangel Michael, asking for protection against manipulation from the dark side because we often don't know what we are dealing with. I woke early the next morning and thought about Cara and how we would pray in Irish together. Cara spoke a cúpla focal, "a couple of words in Irish Gaelic". *Is Mise Cara* (I am Cara) is some of the first Gaelic words she learned. I had a basic grasp of Irish Gaelic while at secondary school, but it drifted over time. I was fortunate to have a brilliant Irish teacher called Ciaran Austin, who encouraged us to use the language often. We were taught the poem 'Is Mise Eire' (I am Ireland) by Patrick Pearse (1879-1916), which Ciaran expected to be told with zest. It began:

"I am Ireland: I am older than the old woman of Beara…". "The "old woman" in the original "cailleach Bheara" is a mysterious figure in Irish myth and folklore. Cailleach in Old Gaelic means 'veiled one', suggesting ancient origins of the wise women or female Druids of pre-Christian, possibly pre-Celtic times. The Lament of the Old Woman of Beare is regarded as one of the finest surviving examples of early Irish verse. She was famed for being the mother and foster mother to at least 50 children who went on to found tribes. Pearse makes that connection and echoes the tone of this 9th c lament – speaking as a female 'I', like in the Lament – only this I is older, she is Ireland" [v].

Cara was a dreamer and loved to hear stories from my school days. For instance, Ciaran's plans to send a school representative (me) from Corpus

Christi College in Belfast to St Paul's Gaelic Athletic Association (GAA) club to participate in an Irish speaking contest. My story was the 'Three Little Pigs' in Gaelic (Na Trì Mucan Beaga). I entered the large hall early one Saturday morning, packed full of fluent Gaelic speakers. After enjoying the Irish dancing and poetry competitions, it was time for the Irish story competition. I wasn't sure about the number of competitors and hoped I'd be last in line and prayed that no one would ask me tricky questions in Gaelic. Within seconds, a lady called me to the stage and, a few minutes later, was applauded off the stage. Away I went, relieved and ready to watch my competitors. After a brief pause, no one else appeared for the storytelling competition, so I was called back on stage to receive a gold medal – a beautiful Gold Fainne. A winner in a contest of one. A black taxi turned up, and the driver started cheering as I told him about the gold. My nieces, nephews and friends' kids are fluent Gaelic speakers, so they'll be cracking up reading this.

We registered our new charity in September 2022. It's great to see other charities, such as Misean Cara - an international and Irish faith-based missionary movement working with some of the most marginalised and vulnerable communities in developing countries. We hope to emulate that.

Man that Stole the Leaf

During the last months of Cara's life, we tried everything to cheer her up. One frequent yarn was an absurd story about a man who stole the leaf. Cara's imagination ran wild, and she laughed uncontrollably at the madness of such a thing happening. To see her switch off from the big stressful world and hoot till her heart was content was priceless.

Approximately one year after her death, I felt low and reminisced about some of the little things that made her happy. While sitting on our bed, I laughed about the man that stole the leaf story. Upon opening my sock drawer, I pulled out a random pair of warm socks on a chilly day in Leeds. Still laughing - I pulled the socks apart but felt something sharp inside one. Right enough, it was a large, fresh green leaf. I took it to Faye, and we both cracked up. Magoo was at her lark again. Crazy little signs seem to happen when you need them.

12

LANA'S CANOE TRAGEDY (SOUTH AFRICA)

By Jeff Fielding in memory of his ex-partner, Lana

> *"We were doing our 6th qualifying race when Lana fell out of the canoe, became trapped under a rock, and drowned. It was the most traumatic day of my life."*

In 2021, I received a message from one of my South African students who'd heard about Cara's story and decided to share his own experience.

"Dear Kieran

I followed the link from LinkedIn to Cara's story. I was moved to tell you my own story.

On the 19th of November 2006, I lost my girlfriend of four years in a boating accident. We had both taken upriver canoe racing as a mixed double team. We were getting more and more competitive each week that went by. There's a famous canoe race in South Africa held over three days and 120km, called the Duzi Canoe Marathon.

It was started by Dr Ian Player, the brother of the golfer Gary Player, in 1951 to commemorate his fallen comrades from World War 2. To qualify for this race, you have to complete six other races.

We were doing our 6th qualifying race when Lana fell out of the canoe, became trapped under a rock, and drowned. It was the most traumatic day of my life. The feeling of helplessness trying to rescue her in a remote wilderness alone and with the river in flood.

Lana's memorial service was on a Thursday at 10 am in the Methodist church in Durban. The first strange occurrence happened to me the following Thursday and continued for a few weeks every Thursday at 10 am. My radio would be overcome by static at 10 am each Thursday. There was an earlier incident in the memorial where a small insect wing came floating down and settled on me, which happened many times over the next few months. As I write this 16 years later, I realise this hasn't happened for many years.

The strangest event was about six weeks after Lana died. I was standing outside my friend's house with another friend called William. My friend's wife (Geraldine) was a good friend of Lana's. It was a sunny morning, and I was still depressed when my phone beeped as an SMS message came through. It was an SMS from Lana saying:

"I am so proud of you; you are so strong".

I was scared and deleted it right away. William saw that I had turned white and asked me what had happened. I told him and then said I had deleted it when he asked to see it. He was then sceptical.

Thirty seconds went by, and the phone beeped again in front of William, and it was the same message. So, we both witnessed the text. It might have been an old message that she had sent me years or months before, and her phone was deactivated and that caused it. The timing and the message seemed significant to me.

I am still trying to understand what it all means. I hope Lana is having the best time in Heaven and loving every day.

I hope you are all well and keeping safe in these Covid times.

Kind regards,

Jeff

Kieran and Faye

One night in 2021, Faye dreamt of picking up her phone and reading out a text message from Cara, who had texted to say:

"Tell Dad I am OK. This world wasn't for me".

I also received signs, such as switching on my phone after Cara died to see a montage of small pictures with Cara and my cousin Constantine. He died of leukaemia shortly before Cara. I had never seen these pictures grouped like that. Included in the photographs was Constantine's father, Costello, who died of a broken heart just weeks after his son's death.

Our dreams continue to merge with reality, which seems incredible. In one, I requested that Lorna Byrne pass her book on to someone in the audience "who needed it". Lorna's gaze was assured and tranquil as she promised to do so. In the same dream, I was in a hotel room and noticed holidaymakers below, stretched out on sun loungers. Then, peering out the narrow window, I saw a large, nasty, blackened face the size of a gable wall. Then, a smaller rounded version drifted in the window before Faye appeared and cupped it in one hand, displaying it in her extended palm.

A small version of the dark energy appeared on the wall. Very sinister. We discussed how these experiences coincided with the launch of our global charity into inequalities and brain disease. Perhaps someone somewhere dislikes our plans to help people and spread messages of hope across religions and faiths.

Another weird dream concerned field rats. A vicious rat attacked an unidentified man. It chewed his throat before Cara appeared. She was looking elongated but young, around seven years old. She jolted the rodent from his neck before securing the space. Everything then seemed brighter and under control as I realised that Cara was intervening in more dreams that involved the dark side. We wonder if the dreams were related to a real-life situation when two dead, putrid rats were found in our garden – front and back.

Little Souls appear around the home

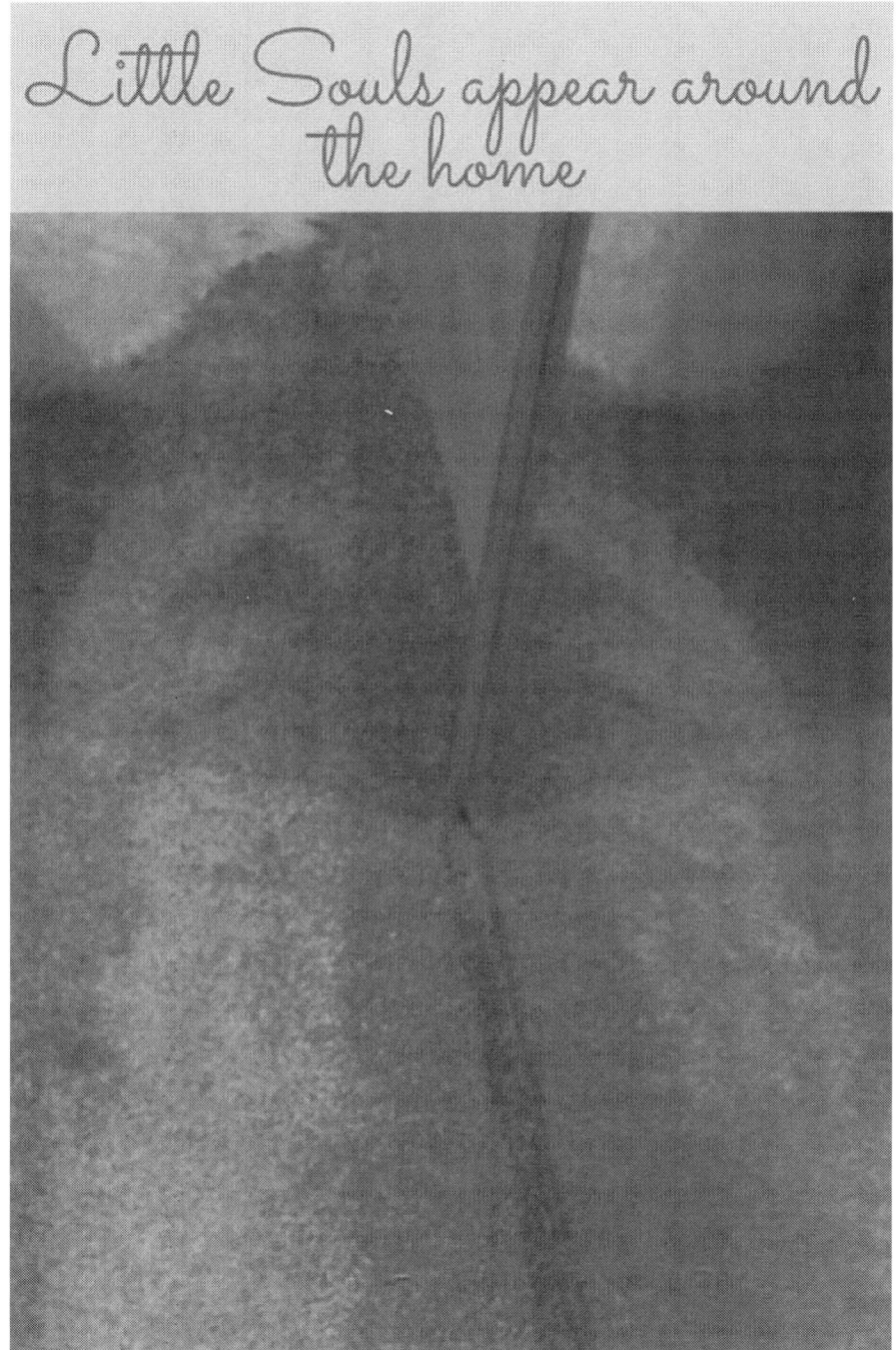

Fig. 16 Little Girl appearing to pray next to Finn

In *Is Mise Cara,* we explain how Cara regularly visited families such as ours and the wider family. For example, my niece Chloe and my mother - (each twice) and through the appearance of supernatural events around each family home. Chloe described significant experiences when she awoke to see Cara sitting at the end of the bed. On both occasions, she wore a white dress with a white flower nestled in her curly hair, white shoes and holding a tiny white purse. Chloe mentioned how Cara didn't speak but just laughed and smiled. She also mentioned gold and white lights surrounding the room. However, Khalid Mukhtar (an international businessman) was the exception of a visit beyond the family...."

"We received a call from Khalid after Lorna's first visit in June 2020. I knew something was amiss by the emotion in his voice. After a few moments, he slowly described a spiritual experience with Cara. We found the call particularly unforgettable because Cara and Khalid had never met. I supervised Khalid on his [management] research project, but we have yet to meet physically"

[The Chapter] 'Khalid's Vision' demonstrates how Cara has appeared in different semblances to people of all faiths and religions. Khalid's mother died around the same time as Cara.

Fig. 17 Khalid Mukhtar's Mother and Father (RIP)

We now explore similar experiences through the chapter on the life and afterlife of 'Dame Julie Iheyinwa Wokocha'.

13

DAME JULIE IHEYINWA WOKOCHA (NIGERIA)

b y Daniel Nuosu in memory of his mother-in-law.

"The [female community] leader stated that Julie visited their Church on the same day she was confirmed dead and requested to hold a seminar with the women of the church".

One may explain the experience of 19th July 2017 as the synchronicities of a lost soul. The late Dame Julie Wokocha went to be with the Lord the day beforehand, after having a stroke. She led a life of dedicated sacrificial service and strategic thinking for the goodwill and comfort of other people. Dame Julie Wokocha was a female leader par excellence, an activist for women's rights and privileges, mobiliser of men, materials, and ideas. Julie was a woman with many excellent attributes, a personality no one could ignore. She was dynamic, prevailing in wisdom, character and intelligence, persuasive in speech and heroic in action, yet humble, considerate, and loving.

Her life touched many segments of society. From villager to the market woman, from the town dweller to those in the church, the government, and traditional institutions.

Fig. 18 Dame Julie Wokocha

Julie's faith in God and dedication to His service were phenomenal. She had a Roman Catholic upbringing but embraced the Anglican doctrine with favour. Some of her contributions to the growth of the church include the following:

- She was a faithful woman leader in All Saints Anglican Church, Samaru, Zaria, 1976-1989.
- The pioneer secretary, Christian Association of Nigeria (CAN), Women's Wing, Kaduna State, Nigeria, 1977-1978.
- As a lay reader, she conducted the first church service in All Saints Anglican Church, World bank Housing Estate, Umuahia, 1978.
- Member of the team led by the Primate Emeritus, Church of Nigeria (Anglican Communion), the Most Rev. Peter J. Akinola, to inspect the suitability of Isuikwuato, Ahaba-Oloko and Arochukwu as Diocesan headquarters for the then proposed Diocese of Isikwuato/Umunneochi, Ikwuano and Arochukwu/Ohafia, 2005.

Julie was well-decorated in the church. Among several certificates and letters of commendation, she received the following awards:

Knight of the order of St Mary, Diocese of Isiala-Ngwa South, 2008.
"Ezinne Ejiagamba" (Mother of Substance) Omoba Archdeaconry, Diocese of Isiala-Ngwa South, 2006.
"Faithful Servant", St. Andrew's Church, Ogbor-Hill, Aba, 2015.
"Conference mother"; World bank Archdeaconry, Diocese of Umuahia, 2016.
Diocesan Trainer in the Women's Ministry of Isiala-Ngwa South. She was at her best during training, seminar or lecture sessions for women.

Dame Julie Wokocha was a vibrant woman who gave birth to five boys and an only daughter (who happens to be my wife, Mrs Ugochi Anne Nwosu) and lived a great life. Julie suddenly took ill in June 2017 without any initial concern of worsening health.

As she received medical care at the Prestigious Federal Medical Center Umuahia, she suddenly relapsed into multiple strokes that kept her bedridden for weeks. Dame Julie Wokocha lost the battle to stroke despite all efforts to keep her alive on the 18th of July 2017. Her remains were deposited in a morgue. Then came this incident that shocked the entire family.

Something significant happened on the day after Julie died on 19th July 2017. A certain women's leader in St. John's Anglican Church, Olokoro, placed a call to one of Julie's daughter-in-law's requesting to speak with Julie. The women leader stated that Julie visited their church the same day she was confirmed dead and requested to hold a seminar with the women of the church.

Julie had instructed her to gather all the church's women for a seminar scheduled for the 19th of July 2017. Julie had also left a mobile number with her with which she could be reached.

The female community leader had gathered the church's women on the scheduled date and placed a call to the mobile number given to her by Dame Julie Wokocha. This mobile number is the mobile number of Dame Julie Wokocha's daughter-in-law.

"The female community leader was shocked when told that the same Dame Julie Wokocha she sought to speak with had been at the morgue for over 24 hours".

Since this bizarre chain of events, many strange thoughts have occupied our minds. Also, after this incident, an elderly family member narrated an experience where he encountered the late Dame Julie Wokocha in a sort of trance, looking very young and beautiful. She advised the man to tell her husband that he should not grieve or trouble himself because she was in a better place.

True to the experience of the elderly family member, Late Dame Julie Wokocha is resting in the bosom of our Lord Jesus Christ. The entire family never stopped loving her and truly believe she is resting in Heaven.

DAME JULIE IHEYINWA WOKOCHA (NIGERIA)

May Julie's Soul and the Souls of all Faithful departed Continue to find rest with God All Mighty.

Amen!!!!

Nwosu Daniel

14

GRANDFATHER FROM MAYO

"Everyone who has even a drop of Irish blood has a special spirituality ingrained within us — a flame that burns deep down within our souls, connecting us to the deep spirituality of our roots." (Lorna Byrne)

Faye and I bumped into a neighbour from our street who offered his condolences about Cara. He was a Derry man who knew Cara from passing and was curious about what happened. We explained that orbs, souls and what appeared to be holy ghosts had frequented our home. After purchasing a copy of *Is Mise Cara*, he was intrigued and shared a story about his own experiences of the afterlife - the day of his grandfather's funeral in County Mayo, Ireland. The family decked the coffin in an Irish tricolour, and he remembered plated food layered around the perimeter of the coffin for visitors to the wake.

Later that day, after the funeral and burial, he recalled how he sat in the kitchen close to the coffin's location. In a daze, he noticed some activity before his grandfather slowly and briefly appeared to him before disappearing. At the time, he was just a young lad, but this proved to be the first of many similar visits from his grandfather.

These experiences continued years after his father, a County Mayo man, and Derry-born mother moved to Leeds. His grandfather was a well-respected man in the community. But the very mention of Cara and the afterlife seemed to have pulled at his heartstrings. He was amazed that we had similar experiences to his own. We, too, found the conversation enlightening simply because it was further proof of the afterlife and offered reassurances about our own experiences.

Since publishing *Is Mise Cara*, many people are still quite reluctant to discuss death and the next stage. But others are less so. Old friends like Jean and Sean contacted me separately to explain how the book had a lasting impact. After losing their faith, they felt more spiritual and at peace with God. So as far as we were concerned, the various messages contained within the fabric of the book resonated far beyond the life of Cara. Many readers have found solace in its intricate messages about God and the afterlife.

In the chapter 'Seeking Alternative Perspectives' (*Is Mise Cara*), Harigo Andri from the 'Salvation Ministry Africa' shared his experiences of paranormal and supernatural experiences. Excerpts below:

"Almost every four or five years, the ghosts appeared to one or both of my parents and told them to exhume their dead bodies (grandparents). My parents practically obeyed accordingly; otherwise, something terrible would happen, like a death in our family. Their ghosts also talked about something good that would happen for my family and to believe when good things happened. This phenomenon was repeated to my parents many times before they submitted to the exhumations due to their fears and beliefs".

15

SIGNS FROM MARTIN (CANADA)

By Jessica in memory of Martin, her husband.

"Martin is relentless and does not stop showing me daily that he is with me, helping me, loving me, and telling me that I need not worry. He shows me that we are still doing life together as partners, just like we intended to when we married. I love my husband forever and always"

My dear husband Martin transitioned into the Spirit World on 27th December 2019, weeks before his 37th birthday. As I type this, we have just passed Martin's second anniversary, and there have been many beautiful signs, synchronicities, and experiences since his crossing. The happenings are mostly with me, but our family and friends have also had their experiences with Martin. This experience is why I am deliberate about using the present tense to refer to my Martin, as he is very much alive and active!

Fig. 19 Jessica with Martin

Martin has always been a lovingly thoughtful, sweet, and funny husband. He continues to guide, provide for, delight me, and much more.

One big example is how I moved to Montreal on a whim. I then effortlessly bought my dream home within a few days of arriving, without having enough money or a job. At this stage, it was only one year after Martin's transition.

My dream home is a real gem. It's a brand-new two-bedroom penthouse condo with a large terrace and gorgeous views of downtown Montreal. The condo is beautifully situated in a vibrant neighbourhood close to shops and amenities yet is still very residential. I'm right by the metro and steps from the Canal where Martin and I used to go biking. Everything I had on my list was checked off and more. Except, it was completely out of my budget!

I was running late when I was on my way to view this condo. So, I was power walking when a bird flew directly in front of me and stopped me in my tracks. Then another bird appeared. For two birds to stop me like that is akin to me running last minute in front of a speeding truck!

I stopped and blinked. I said loudly: "Hello, birds, I am late; please let me pass!" and tried to push through them. Usually, when you walk towards birds, they move aside. Not these birds; they wouldn't budge. Something inside me told me to relax, pause, and enjoy the company of the birds. So, I did. The two birds were looking directly at me. They held me there for two minutes - an eternity when you were running late! I stood there, admiring them. I love birds, and so does Martin.

I knew it was a sign from Martin. I thought he was saying, "Hi! I'm here with you!" but later I realised he was telling me that the condo I was about to see was 'The One'. Yes, the condo was very nice, and I loved it! But unfortunately, it was out of my price range.

With not enough money and no job, it just wasn't feasible. As a new young "widow", I knew I had to be careful as Martin's death left me insecure about my finances. So, it's strange that I put in an offer on this gorgeous condo a few days later. After a little back and forth, the seller and I agreed on a price that was less than his asking but still way over my budget! It would take another ten days for me to settle the financing. Somehow, in those ten days, everything clicked, and suddenly I could afford to not only buy the condo but also carry the costs!!!

The banks were not willing to lend me money. Still, one credit union agreed and gave me an offer even more competitive than the banks. Please note that Canadian institutions are very conservative. Someone like me - with no job and no credit score (because I had lived abroad with Martin!) - is NOT a suitable candidate. My mortgage broker at the credit union asked me two questions: 1) Do you have a job? No. 2) Do you want to get a job? Yes. It took him a few days to push the papers through and give me an answer.

During those days, I was trying not to stress. I went for a walk. I was in a park when again, two birds flew directly in front of me, really fast. They cut me off abruptly but didn't stop flying. I followed the birds with my eyes and watched them gather other birds to form a swarm. Martin loves birds flying in a swarm, and he would point them out to me whenever he saw them.

I noticed the swarm get big in the sky and was surprised at how many birds there were (where did they all come from?). Suddenly and unexpectedly, the swarm of birds ALL descended upon me! They surrounded me from all sides! I instinctively shielded my face with my arms and could feel their wings brush against me. That's how close they were! What's interesting is that there was someone nearby who was feeding the squirrels, yet the birds formed around me! I was a little nervous about the birds.

But there was a man who had seen the swarm engulf me, and he approached the edge of my bird bubble to assure me that everything was fine and that the birds were not dangerous. I stood there in awe and glee at what was happening.

My mortgage broker let me know I was approved a few days later. I closed on my condo a month later. I've been living in my dream home for a year, and it's been incredible!!! The neighbours and neighbourhood are even better than I expected. My home gives me comfort, stability, safety, security, joy, and pride. It is also a great investment, which will help me in the future.

All of these feelings are what I felt being with Martin. He knew what I wanted and needed and helped me buy this home. There are so many details in this story that are related to Martin. But the birds are the most striking and most beautiful!

Martin is relentless and does not stop showing me daily that he is with me, helping me, loving me, and telling me that I need not worry. He shows me that we are still doing life together as partners, just like we intended to when we married. I love my husband forever and always.

Kieran and Faye

See *Is Mise Cara* (see pictures on the www.carabraindiseasefoundation.com website and @caramiamervyn Instagram account). Snapshot below.

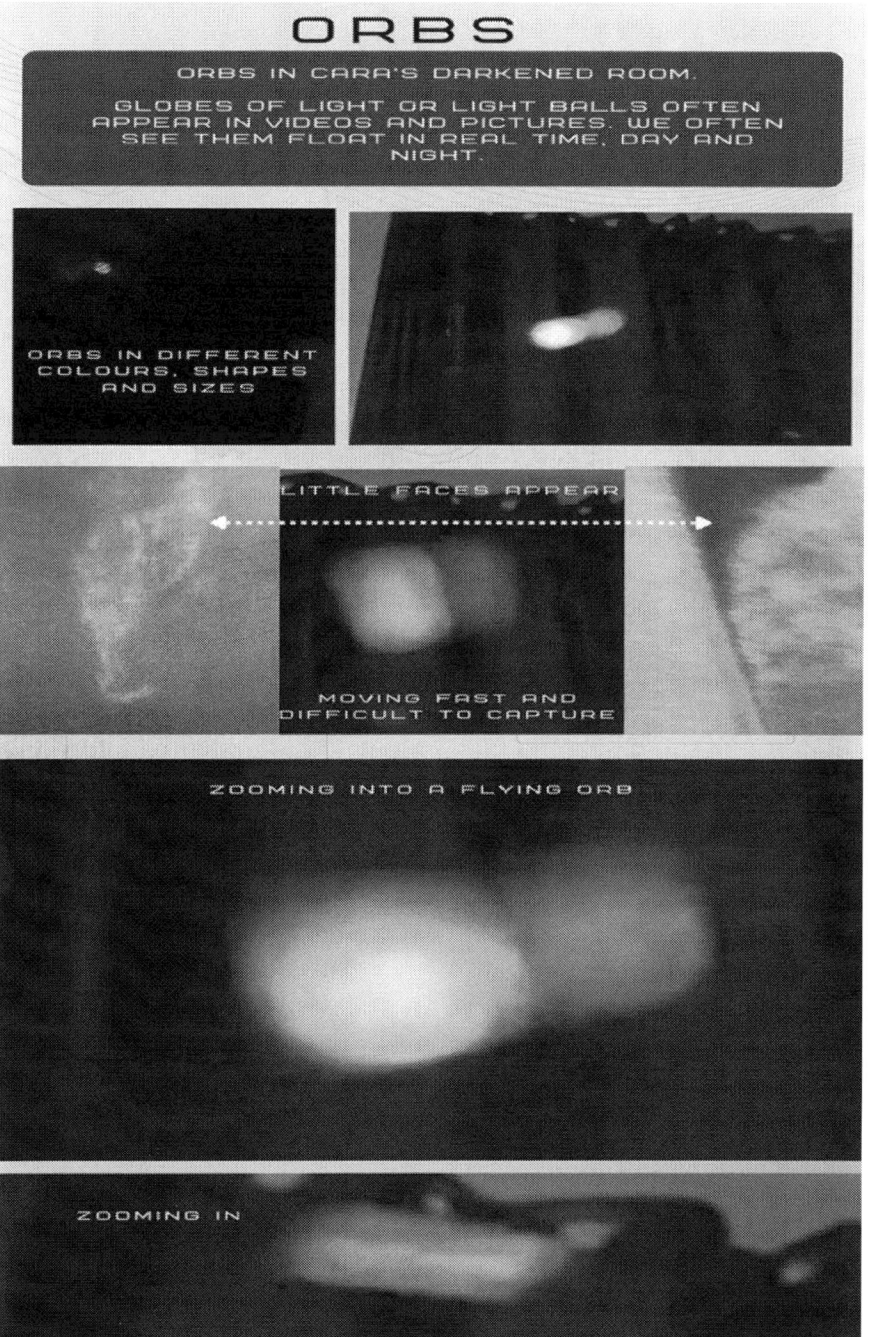

Fig. 20 Faces and Orbs

In *Is Mise Cara,* we describe many vivid dreams. These dreams seemed to merge with reality. These continue to this day. On the right is an example of the types of orbs we see floating around our homes and beyond. They tend to follow us. We witness and then dream about the orbs regularly, which seems significant on many levels.

One afternoon in March 2022, Faye went to collect Finn from school. First, the flickers appeared, then the clear orbs as I attempted to complete a short YouTube workout in the living room. I followed one orb hovering at the corner of the ceiling before observing in silence. After a few moments, I was compelled to reach out toward the shimmering figure but felt an icy chill the closer I got.

As if someone had opened the freezer door on a mild March Day in Leeds. Suddenly, my right hand felt pierced as if stung by a wasp—a painful and uncomfortable experience accompanied by pins and needles. I ran around the living room wondering what had just happened but simultaneously having a good idea. My hand doubled in size - populated by peculiar purple and red patches before slowly returning to normal just as Faye and Finn returned home. Sensing danger, it felt like I'd entered the unwelcome territory.

Lorna advises how souls are so pure that we should never approach or reach out - so it's a lesson learned. Lorna Byrne describes her own experiences, e.g., when she encountered a recently departed person whose soul has not fully transitioned to Heaven.

We wrote the early sections of *Is Mise Cara* from our back garden in Leeds. Early on Easter Sunday morning, 2020, we noticed a beautiful wood pigeon lying dead beneath the garden patio table.

We disposed of the bird, but scores of exquisite white feathers remained on the grass for weeks afterward.

SIGNS FROM MARTIN (CANADA)

> "One possibility is that it hit the back window close to Cara's favourite seat, and a magpie may have plucked it? But there was no blood on the bird or marks on the window, just a mass of feathers".

Since Cara's passing, we have captured orbs dancing around wood pigeons outside Cara's window on several occasions. Three birds appeared directly outside the window as Finn and I prayed in Cara's room. Cara's friend's mum spotted a pure white dove fly over our house on the day of Cara's funeral. As we left the hospital with family after Cara had passed, a flock of birds flew across to us and started to follow us down the street. My brother Damien asked if they were for us. And as we walked through the Robin Eccup reservoir, a robin appeared each time we talked about Cara. And followed us around the reservoir and occasionally flew between us.

In *Is Mise Cara*, we refer to numerous experiences of white feathers appearing inside and outside the home, often as someone mentions Cara's name. We visited Leeds City Centre one Saturday afternoon for Mother's Day presents. On route through town, the first of three white feathers appeared. One white feather drifted and dropped at our feet as we crossed the bridge beside the LGI hospital while talking about Cara. Roughly an hour afterwards, a beautiful white feather drifted from above and landed squarely on Finn's chest. Then, as we approached the car to return home, another feather drifted down and landed on Faye. On the drive home, we discussed how the angels probably reached out to say that all was okay. That Cara was looking out for us. I'm a gambling man, apart from the occasional football bet on a Saturday.

As my Da often says, "You'll never see a skint bookie" [bookmaker]). But I'm pretty sure that Paddy Power would have serious odds on a feather landing on or around us at three locations within a 2-mile radius in a short period.

Lorna Byrne acknowledges that white feathers stem from birds. However, it's the timing and significance of their landing. Lorna sees it as a special gift from the angels. For instance, I remember itching as I worked on a project in my office while also thinking about Cara. After scratching my face, I realised that somehow a white feather appeared stuck to my cheek. How could that be possible? The same happened to Faye's mum, who searched her home looking for a white feather that she found and appeared to have lost but was in a similar spot.

16

ASYA RIP JUNE 2022 [ISTANBUL]

Written by mum, Merve Duran

"Cara and my Asya are working for us in Heaven. We have not lost our beautiful daughters; they have not disappeared. They only moved from this temporary place to a permanent home. Until we move on and are together, I'm praying that the signs continue from them both".

Dear Faye and Kieran.

Firstly, I would like to thank you for making me feel that I'm not alone in this world. I am very grateful that you include our Asya and our story in your beautiful daughter "Cara's" book. I always say that our beautiful daughters are working for us in Heaven.

My Asya was diagnosed with a brain tumour (DIPG) on the 10th of June 2021. After fighting it for a year, my beautiful daughter, my "Snow White", moved on to the other realm on the 10th of June 2022.

From the first day my Asya was born, she was very different (exceptional). Her beauty, gaze, attitude and behaviour would take my breath away, and everyone noticed her grace. She departed from this world (realm) with grace.

Burials are a key part of our religious beliefs. Physical bodies that no longer function meets the earth together with their souls and remain there until we meet again.

I never believed that my Asya's soul was in the ground. Thankfully, according to our religious beliefs, children who move on before puberty, by the judgment of Allah, go to Heaven and remain with Allah. Therefore, I believe that this Heaven is the garden (grave) of my Asya. What matters is the soul, which remains with us forever. Even if we cannot see and touch them, despite desperately wanting to hug them and miss them so much, their souls are always with us.

Yes, it is very tough for the heart in our physical bodies not to be able to hug and touch our loved ones. Every time this heaviness sinks into my heart, Asya's signs turn my bleeding heart into a flower bed, thank God.

Following Asya's funeral, while sitting in our living room with our loved ones, a ladybird flew into the room and remained with us for several hours. Every time I went to Asya's garden, I saw a ladybird. I was having breakfast and chatting with my friend while simultaneously thinking of Asya. From the depth of my heart, I prayed to Allah for another sign. After finishing my daily tasks, I visited my daughter's garden. While there, a purple flower appeared to me as if it was smiling. At that moment, I felt like I was taking the flower from my Asya. While taking a picture, a ladybird flew into my palm and remained there for quite a while.

One day a ladybird appeared from between the grapes that had been in the fridge for days. It was moving very slowly as it seemed unwell. We put it amongst the leaves of our house plant. It lived with us for a few days. Later, I sadly found its dead body while cleaning the house. While cleaning the rest of the rooms, I noticed another ladybird crawling on the carpet, which looked very healthy. It crawled onto my hand and flew and danced inside the house. It was beautiful.

My daughter is still telling me many things and teaching me many things. This trait has always been special about her. She did not pass through this life in vain.

A passage from the Holy Qur'an I chose randomly reads as follows:

"We rejoined the child with the mother so that the poor woman's heart is full of joy and her pain is removed for a little while, for her to see for herself that Allah's promise was genuine. Within this separation, there is eternal beauty towards the future. However, many people are not aware of this."
Kasas Suresi 13. Ayet (Chapter) from the Qur'an

Asya was sedated during the last weeks of her life. The hospital consultant limited my visiting times to certain parts of each day. Just a few hours before she passed away, they took my husband and me inside to see her. At that moment, as I was hugging and kissing her, I smelt a different scent.

"My God, was this the smell of death?" I said to myself because this scent was not one, I had ever smelt before. Nowadays, I sense this scent unexpectedly, especially when thinking of her. In those instances, I say **"My dear Asya, are you here" and I cry with joy.**

This scent is unexplainable; I cannot say that it is similar to this, that, or anything like "this is the best fragrance in the world" or compare it to anything else. It is a scent my Asya left me as she was departing, and now from time to time, this special scent makes me feel that she is always with me.

I get different signs at different times. When she was physically with us and we were preparing breakfast together, we often put some birdseed in front of the kitchen window. Ever since she departed, a baby bird has come to the window from time to time. One day, Asya's beloved brother Ayaz and I were having breakfast with pain in our hearts, missing Asya's presence at the table. Suddenly, a baby bird appeared at the window and observed us. We got up and put some seeds out, and normally the birds flew away; however, this one stayed at the window. While feeding, two bigger birds came and scared away the little one. When I returned to the window, the two big birds flew away, but the little one remained and only flew off after it finished feeding.

It has been 127 days since my beautiful Asya departed, and the signs I have been getting were these so far.

Cara and my Asya are working for us in Heaven. We have not lost our beautiful daughters; they have not disappeared. They only moved from this temporary place to a permanent home. Until we move on and are together, I'm praying that the signs continue from them both.

With love,

Merve Duran and my beautiful daughter Asya Duran.

Kieran and Faye

These experiences, e.g. with birds, resonate with our own after Cara passed. On the 16th of June 2022, I asked Cara for a sign before going on the school run. I told her that she would give me loads of guidance anyway and not to worry if not. Later that afternoon, Faye asked Cara for a sign too. As we sat in the garden on this hot June day, I noticed a small pigeon sitting on the roof. We began to joke that it was probably Cara in disguise. It briefly stared us out before floating down and circling us both.

The cool wind spun from its fluttered wings before it landed gracefully upon Faye's head. See Instagram video @caramiamervyn. It remained there for approximately 10 minutes. The bird then hung around, spending the afternoon peeping and tapping the window next to Cara's seat. We then spotted some unmistakable clear orbs hovering around the bird, which assured us it was Cara.

Fig. 21 Finn and Faye with our pigeon visitors

At one stage, it seemed to have gone, so I went back to my computer and googled 'why do pigeons tap a window' before reading some biblical interpretations. Simultaneously, the window tapped again; sure enough, it was the pigeon.

As Faye left to collect Finn from school, I played a YouTube boxing video on my phone and worked out at the side of the house. Sensing someone was watching, I turned to see that the bird had followed me around the house and just sat, staring motionless as I worked on the bag. I correctly suspected that it would stick around to see Finn.

Within minutes, it circled Finn, who'd just returned home like a long-lost friend, before floating above his head and gently landing. It stayed for a few minutes, looking like it had served its mission before drifting back to the roof and off to the trees.

We haven't stopped talking about that bird and its similarities to Jessica's story. What were the chances? This experience reminds me of a famous poem called "The Raven" from 1845 about a man devastated over the recent death of his wife. Excerpts below…

POEMS

The Bird (Faye Mervyn)

If I had one moment with you, I don't know what I'd say?
I'd take you to the beach and hope you didn't fly away.
I'd sit you down and tell you that I loved you very much. You made me smile oh so, so much.
But as the sun begins to set, I realise it's time, time for you to fly away because you are no longer mine.
As I watch you from a distance, I see you fly away
I hope that you don't forget me and return to me one day.
Love Mum and Dad.

ASYA RIP JUNE 2022 [ISTANBUL]

The Raven - Edgar Allan Poe [vi]

Once upon a midnight dreary, while I pondered, weak and weary,
Over many a quaint and curious volume of forgotten lore—

While I nodded, nearly napping, suddenly, there came a tapping,
As of someone gently rapping, rapping at my chamber door.
"'Tis some visitor," I muttered, "tapping at my chamber door—

Only this and nothing more."

Ah, distinctly, I remember it was in the bleak December;
And each separate dying ember wrought its ghost upon the floor.

Eagerly I wished the morrow;—vainly, I had sought to borrow

From my books surcease of sorrow—sorrow for the lost Lenore—
For the rare and radiant maiden whom the angels name Lenore—

Nameless here for evermore.

And the silken, sad, uncertain rustling of each purple curtain
Thrilled me—filled me with fantastic terrors never felt before;
So that now, to still the beating of my heart, I stood repeating

"'Tis some visitor entreating entrance at my chamber door—
Some late visitor entreating entrance at my chamber door;—

This it is and nothing more."

Presently my soul grew stronger; hesitating then no longer,
"Sir," said I, "or Madam, truly your forgiveness I implore;

But the fact is I was napping, and so gently you came rapping,
And so faintly you came tapping, tapping at my chamber door,
That I scarce was sure I heard you"—here I opened wide the door;—

Darkness there and nothing more.

Deep into that darkness, peering, long I stood there wondering, fearing,
Doubting, dreaming dreams no mortal ever dared to dream before;
But the silence was unbroken, and the stillness gave no token,
And the only word there spoken was the whispered word, "Lenore?"
This I whispered, and an echo murmured back the word, "Lenore!"—
Merely this and nothing more...

17

DION JUDE HUTCHINGS (NEW YORK)

by Linda Badamo and Alana Hutchings

"Dion has since come to us many times through these songs. Dion's love of music lives on through these moments, as I know he is with us. With the most impeccable timing, songs such as "Spirit In The Sky" or "While My Guitar Gently Weeps" will come on the radio".

Fig. 22 Dion Hutchings, RIP

"Dion's mum Linda attended a psychic reading in the United States in 2022. Dion shared the message that he 'knew about the little girl from Leeds [Cara] with the brain tumour' and how he was very proud of Linda and Alana for writing this chapter in Signs from Cara and Beyond. Another incredible message from the Spirit World".

On 17th November 2020, I lost my 26-year-old son, Dion Jude Hutchings. Little did I know that I would start receiving beautiful messages and signs from my son in Heaven. I soon learned that there is a thin veil between us here on Earth and in the afterlife.

It all started that night when my daughter, Alana, was coming home on a flight from California. I had to break the news to her over text. She alerted the crew, and they quickly mobilised to get her off the plane as soon as they landed—the kind and quick-to-act staff announced to get Alana off the plane immediately. A very compassionate flight attendant sat next to Alana before landing. Alana was stunned after the name on her badge read, "Angel".

After getting her baggage and starting on her way home, Alana was still in shock. Just then, an unfamiliar song came over the radio. She knew it was a sign. A van pulled up beside them, and Alana couldn't help but notice the array of guitar-themed stickers on the back, such as Fender, Gibson and stickers shaped like guitar picks. My son was a talented guitarist whose passion for music was known by everyone. Alana knew this was the start of the signs from her brother.

When she got home, she remembered a few lyrics from the song she heard in the car, which made her think of Dion. We discovered that it was called "Heaven Beside You" by a grunge rock group, Alice In Chains. Neither she nor I were familiar with this band or their music, but we later learned that this was one of my son's favourite rock groups.

Dion's father was with him a few days before his passing. He told us a song came on the radio, and Dion exclaimed, "Alice in Chains! They're one of my favourite groups!" We wonder if that was the same song that played for Alana during that car ride home. We bet it was.

On 19th November 2020, Alana got a message from one of her close friends, who is very spiritual and even offers Tarot Card readings. She lit a candle and said a prayer for Dion. After connecting with him, she told my mom and me to seek something specific in his belongings.

"Something small, shiny. Maybe a piece of jewellery. Blue and gold. Look for blue and gold."

Alana and I were surprised as we hadn't noticed anything similar in his items. "Keep it close", Alana's friends said. Soon…this would all come to fruition. In the days after my son's passing, I went through a drawer of his possessions. Among the items in the drawer, there was nothing that appeared unusual. It didn't dawn on me that I had found a tiny gold heart locket charm and put it in a box on top of the dresser.

Later that night, I had a revelation that caused me to realise I had found what my son was trying to tell me. The tiny gold locket I found didn't belong to any of us, and I'd never seen it before. I didn't think anything of it and put it inside a blue box on the dresser. The box the heart was placed in was royal blue with a gold seal on the bottom of it. I couldn't believe it! I know this was the message from my son that Alana's friend referenced that night. I "keep it close" as I added it to the cross necklace I wear daily. This was just the start of beautiful unexplainable moments that I know I have my son to thank for.

Dion's Wake

On the day of my son's wake, his presence became known, and many occurrences happened. Dion was a talented guitarist, lyricist, poet, and welder. As a tribute to my son's musical talent, we inscribed the Beatles song title "While My Guitar Gently Weeps" on the inside of his casket. It was a beautiful tribute and fully displaced Dion's guitar collection. My boyfriend's daughter, Heather, met us there that night and earlier gifted us a beautiful angel portrait she made in honour of Dion. We put the picture on display at the wake. On her neck, she wore a diamond guitar charm necklace that we had given her years before. Heather wore this to remember him by. When Heather paid her respects to Dion, she was taken aback to realise that she recognised the Beatles quote we had embroidered along his casket. She exclaimed, "I just heard that song playing on the way here!" I knew Dion was saying thank you for her painting and wearing the guitar necklace in his memory.

Starting that night, I was reminded that "there are no coincidences". These moments reminded us that our loved ones are closer than we could imagine.

There was an intermission between the viewing that night at the wake. While our guests had dinner upstairs, I entered the room to be alone with my son. I wanted to play some of Dion's favourite songs while I sat there with him. In my youth, I sang and acted and was quite talented. I performed at various clubs and was known for my singing and acting talent. One of my favourite songs to achieve with my pianist was "Send in the Clowns". I was amazed when this song came on over the room's speaker system as soon as I entered. As I was alone, speaking to my son, two of my close friends came to check on me. We sat together as I cried and chatted with my son. Suddenly, the lights began to flicker on and off above us gently. They flashed repeatedly, and my friends and I knew Dion was with us.

Dion's Funeral

The day of Dion's funeral started with numerous signs from him. We were up early before we had to say our goodbyes at the funeral home. We were painfully silent and were dreading making this final drive to say our goodbyes. Out of nowhere, Dion's car parked out front started blasting its alarm. I was a nervous wreck and had to fish to the bottom of my bag to turn it off. We took that as a sign to leave early and started making our way. As we drove on the expressway, at 7:11 am, the song on the radio played "Spirit In The Sky". We were blessed with the most beautiful sunrise I have ever seen that morning. The next song on the radio was "Hey Jude" (Remember, Dion's middle name is Jude). If Dion's car alarm didn't mysteriously go off when it did, we might not have left in time to marvel at the gorgeous sunrise and hear those special two songs. As I said, there are no coincidences.

Dion has since come to us many times through these songs. Dion's love of music lives on through these moments, as I know he is with us. With the most impeccable timing, songs such as "Spirit In The Sky" or "While My Guitar Gently Weeps" will come on the radio. "Hey, Jude" and "Knockin' On Heaven's Door" are two others that always seem to find us.

Father Tom delivered a beautiful eulogy at Dion's funeral service about my son. He concluded with a favourite quote of his by Winnie the Pooh:

"You are braver than you believe, stronger than you seem, smarter than you think and loved more than you know".

I was crying in the pew, fully aware I recognised that quote from somewhere.

On the way home from the cemetery, once again, was a breath-taking sky. Never in my life, in one day, have I witnessed such a beautiful sunrise and sunset as we saw that day. The sky's radiance looked like it was opening its gates for Heaven's newest arrival. I had to fetch my phone to take pictures of this sunset. Amazingly, as I looked at the photos, each image had small, turquoise-coloured orbs. It was a beautiful memory that I will have forever.

A Package from my Cousin

A few days later, I received a package in the mail from my cousin. It was a plaque with the Winnie the Pooh quote recited at Dion's funeral service. He left a note saying: "I think Dion would want you to have this". Suddenly, I realised why the quote was so familiar to me. A few days before Dion's death, I saw an ad for a chrome bracelet engraved "To my son", followed by the above quote. I was touched by it and considered buying it for Dion and sent him a photo of it. I found it remarkable that I sent Dion this quote two days before he passed, and somehow, he found a way to have it sent back to me. What are the chances that the priest would say this EXACT quote I sent my son a few days prior? Then, my cousin sent me the plaque with the exact quote, insisting Dion would want me to have it. Every time I opened my phone for the next few months, the same quote would appear on name tags, clocks, jewellery, and countless other gift items.

I know it was my son, Dion, coming through to tell me that I was strong enough to go through this, and he was by my side.

The Music Box

The next story I'm about to share touched me ever so much. It was Good Friday, and I was upstairs making Easter baskets. As I made them, I talked to Dion and told him how much I wished he was here. I also told him I wished I had made him an Easter basket. I went downstairs and watched television with my daughter, Alana and my boyfriend, Joe. Suddenly, Joe asked, "Do you hear that music?" We said no? what music? He muted the tv, and we froze when we heard a soft tune playing upstairs. We followed the song we heard up the stairs to another room. We walked into the upstairs room where I had just been making Easter baskets to hear a tune still playing, the sound of a music box. We searched the room, not knowing where the source of the familiar tune was coming from. Under a piece of furniture piled in dust was a music box that I didn't realise was even there. The song playing was the tune of "It's a wonderful world".

As I picked up the dusty music box, I was amazed to read what was inscribed on top of it. It read…

"MOTHER, YOU ARE AN ANGEL WHO HOLDS ME UP WHEN I FIND IT HARD TO FLY."

Instantly, I started to cry. I realised Dion had heard me while making the Easter gifts and speaking to him. You have to understand a music box CAN NOT play unless it is sufficiently wound from the bottom or fully opened from the top. This box had been seen or touched for a while. Neither was it wound up nor opened. Somehow, someway, the music had played for us. Once again, I don't believe in coincidences. Since then, we've heard "It's a wonderful world" playing at frequent, opportune moments and can't help but smile.

Camille (RIP)

The final story I will share involves my mother, Camille. My mother was a beautiful woman inside and out. My mother had a way of getting you with her Italian guilt. She would tell me numerous times:

"Linda, when I die, you have to promise me to play these two songs". The songs she wanted to have played at her funeral were "My Sweet Lord" and "Oh Happy Day".

I assured her that we would find a way to accommodate her final wishes. One weekend, Alana and I planned on doing some errands to continue with the story. My phone rang as we walked out of the house and into the car. It was my mom. She asked me, "Why is everyone getting signs from Dion except me?" She was adamant about receiving her special sign. I laughed and told her, "Okay, Mom, I'll see what I can do".

I spoke out loud to Dion, saying, "Please give your grandma her sign! She's driving me crazy!" When I hung up the phone and started the car, "My Sweet Lord" was playing on the radio. Alana and I couldn't believe the timing of this song. I thought to myself, "Thanks, Dion! You work fast!" I called my mom right back to tell her. However, she still insisted, "No, Linda, I want my sign!" Apparently, another sign from my son would have to be sent directly to my mother.

Rose with Black Thorns

That night, an impending storm was on the way. It was the kind of storm you get updates that power lines could be down, resulting in outages. To preface this night, my son left behind numerous notebooks of his writing and poetry. I used one of Dion's poems on the back of his mass card with his photo. I will share it below:

> *I'm just a rose with a Black Thorn*
> *in the middle of a Rainstorm*
> *Do you think we can be Reborn,*
> *if things get too worn & torn?*
> *It is quite a sighting,*
> *but if you find it frightening,*
> *Just hold my hand thru the*
> *thunder & lightning!*
> *Just a Rose in the thundering Rain,*
> *So much beauty, So much pain.*
> *Watch as the sky cries for me,*
> *The simplicity of serenity*

> *is the only Remedy!*
> *I know it's calling me,*
> *but I don't hear a sound.*
> *The urge to get high*
> *above the clouds.*
> *I feel it pulling me-*
> *don't let it drag me down!*
> *I feel it pulling me,*
> *watch me leave the ground!*
> *The silence is deafening,*

but it's so loud...

Now, for the conclusion of the story...

My mother calls us the night of the storm. She excitedly tells us, "I got my sign!" She explains to us she was sitting in the kitchen beside her window when she noticed a large box outside. Along the side of the box read "Perishables", and it was getting soaked in the Rain. She got her coat and went out in the rainstorm to retrieve the now soggy box. She assumed it was a gift basket sent from a friend.

As my mother opened the box, there were beautiful roses in a vase with blackthorns left on the stems. The vase included a sticker that read:

"Dear client, your roses have thorns. Please handle with care. Removing the thorns will shorten the vase's life". So, we've opted to leave the thorns intact. Thank you."

My mother was ecstatic. This was the sign she had been waiting for from my son. "Linda, it's just like his poem. He sent me roses with blackthorns in the middle of a rainstorm!" We all were teary-eyed at this magnificent sign from above.

Unfortunately, we received shocking news about five months after Dion's

passing. My dear mother, Camille, suddenly passed away unexpectedly. Dion's death took a toll on her. She returned to Heaven, reunited with him and my father. Also, if you are wondering if I played the two songs she wanted at her funeral, we did!

After my mother's passing, there have been many more signs that SHE has shown us. I know, without a doubt, that her grandson is showing her the ropes. My mom's signs have been amazing, and that would be another few chapters, my dear friends! Just remember, our loved ones truly are around us. Keep your heart and mind open to the signs and messages they may bestow upon you. I am forever blessed with the signs my family and I have received. I always say, "There's no such thing as coincidences!"

I have received so many signs from my son, mother and father that I started an Instagram account to showcase Dion's talents and these signs from above. **@ONEMOTHERSMISSION.**

Kieran and Faye

We had a similar experience to Linda's, with lights flickering as we prayed over Cara at Slaters Funeral Home in Leeds. Her body lay directly below the lights in an open casket. The funeral director mentioned how she had never experienced the lights flicker before. In I*s Mise Cara* (see chapter 'Ashes and The Emerald Angel'), we discuss the funeral director's experience of music associated with her late husband. Cara's favourite song then began to play as we drove home with Cara's ashes. Such a surreal experience.

Dion's mum Linda attended a psychic reading in the United States in 2022. At the end, Dion shared a message to say that he 'knew about the little girl from Leeds with the brain tumour' and how he was very proud of Linda and Alana for writing this chapter in Signs from Cara and Beyond. Another incredible message from the Spirit World.

Immediately after hearing about Linda's experience, I added Dion's picture to the manuscript while listening to the United Stand (Manchester United YouTube fan site).

Suddenly, the feed stopped and was replaced by an advertisement. After clicking 'skip ad,' a song started to play instead of the United Stand. Guess what song?
'While My Guitar Gently Weeps.'

I laughed and said 'fair play big lad; I hear ya'.

18

ANN'S SIGNS (AUSTRALIA/USA)

by Ann R. Neal in memory of her parents, George and Ethel

I like to think of synchronicity as where Heaven and Earth converge. It can happen very simply or profoundly. No matter what way, you are left with a sense of wonder and surprise. For you realise God, Divine Beings, and His universe and all within it have overlapped for a brief period of your time. The natural and the supernatural are made evident. There is no doubt that Teilhard de Chardin was correct in writing:

"We are not human beings having a spiritual experience but are spiritual beings having a human experience".

The wondrous and meaningful synchronicities happen through our heart with the eyes of our spirit, being present to God and aware of the spiritual world around us, and being open to see what IS there. Synchronicity is simply seeing the miracles. It is also a reminder of something bigger, mysterious, benevolent, and loving BEYOND humanity. And that is very humbling and fills me with great joy!

I was born in Sydney, Australia, as a fifth-generation Australian and the younger born of identical twins. Spiritually I have always been connected to God and knew angels existed at an early age. At the age of five years, I was separated from friends at a shopping mall and knew I was lost, but I also knew my way home. I had to walk five miles, and the angels helped me navigate, crossing a major intersection alone and getting home safely.

At the age of twenty-one years, I became a follower of Jesus Christ. My twin and I became believers at the same time. We were hungry for truth and submerged ourselves for the next ten months absorbing God's word and praying for long hours. We did not attend church until after the first six months. We relied on the Holy Spirit for divine teaching, instruction, and counsel. Our hearts were on fire. Our faces were radiant. We were fully alive for the first time. I am very thankful for the gift of becoming a believer as a young adult. I could own my faith and build an intimate, personal relationship with God through Jesus Christ. My passion for spiritual truth has never left me.

Synchronicity first impacting on Ann's Awareness.

Shortly after my first year of intense biblical study, my faith was immediately put into action. I became a Flight Attendant (with my twin) and witnessed God answering prayer daily. As a domestic and later international Flight Attendant, I was required to be out in the cabin after the meal service. This may be where synchronicity first began to impact my awareness. I noticed the people I encountered often left a deep imprint from their message, or I was to help or encourage them.

One day, my twin sister and I travelled the forty-five-minute drive to the airport; we were almost in a deadly car accident. A taxi driver suddenly pulled into our single lane from a side street on the opposite side of the road. I swerved to miss the oncoming car but could see no room to move over. The kerb was right there, and a telephone pole. Miraculously we seemed to pass right through the pole and avoid disaster. Heaven and Earth converged at this time in a potent synchronicity.

Another Synchronicity

Another example was when my twin and I took leave without pay for a month and travelled to Europe to meet up with our older brother. He was the one who had radically been converted to Christianity through Campus Crusade while in his final year of Architecture at university. My brother challenged our family to read the bible and make a decision. We travelled by train all day and night in a sleeper cabin.

We had no money as we were waiting for our destination, still three hours away, to cash traveler's cheques. We awoke to our brother being ravenous and had no food left. I prayed to God, asking Him to please help us. Within ten minutes, there was a knock at our cabin door. I opened it to see a man standing there apologetically explaining they had an extra breakfast tray, and if we would like it.
I can still envision the astounding look of wonder, marvel, surprise, joy, and thanksgiving on my brother's face. Synchronicity!

Ann meeting her husband

People love hearing the story of how my husband and I met. It is a story full of synchronicities. The same brother I had travelled through Europe with ended up staying at a Christian centre called L'Abri in England. He met, fell in love with, and proposed to his future wife, who lived in Chicago, USA. This meeting happened over two weeks, and they were married a year later in the USA, where they began married life.

I had been dating a fellow Flight attendant for several months. I had experienced a Godly nudging that the relationship would not work. I had begun my annual six-week vacation. My boyfriend, currently working on a twenty-one-day trip through Europe, suggested I wait to come and join him as planned. Rather, I should fly to meet him at his last port before returning to Sydney. I knew something suspicious was going on. It was a red flag. I decided it was time to end the relationship. I called my brother in Chicago and asked if I could escape Sydney by visiting him for a couple of weeks. He said yes. I cried for three days, packed my bag and boarded my twenty-hour flight feeling devastated and unlikely to marry again. I was almost twenty-seven years of age (whilst growing up in Sydney, New South Wales, at that time, had a three-to-one ratio of girls to boys). My father liked to tell my twin and me that we would probably remain unmarried like his 'maiden' twin aunts).

I remember telling God my life was in His hands as I prepared 'to jump off a cliff into the great unknown.' My life as I knew it was about to change in ways I could never have foreseen. This was my first trip to Chicago alone. Before it, I had always visited with my twin.

As I drove into my brother's driveway on my day of arrival, I noticed a nice-looking young man working on the house next door. The house was an old Victorian 'Painted Lady' and was beautiful. Unbeknownst to me at the time, this builder, who was working his way through college, had placed a single ad for carpentry work in one newspaper. Three months had passed before he got a call (the only call), an interview and the job to do restoration work on the old house. He had been there for several weeks. During this time, my architect brother had become interested in the project and had become acquainted with the builder, Doug.

I met Doug three days after arriving. Nine days later, we were engaged. Almost a year after I had left my flying job, moved my scant belongings across the world, married and lived in the middle of the USA. This chance encounter was God converging Heaven and Earth. There is divine power in synchronicity. I knew I would marry Doug before he knew anything about me. It was a highly charged spiritual

encounter.

Today we celebrate almost thirty-five years of marriage with four children and six grandchildren. I have lived almost longer in the USA than in Australia. Our marriage has endured illness, financial ruin, and numerous moves both across the world and back. It has also experienced long periods of being separated from my Australian family. Yet, I know that the first synchronistic encounter was the foundation on which our marriage has stood the test of time.

After living for six years in Chicago's western suburbs, Doug decided to get his Master of Divinity Degree in Sydney, Australia. We packed our belongings and moved our young family back to Sydney. During the next four years, synchronicity occurred many times in unexpected ways. We lived below the poverty level while on a government-funded student assistance programme at college. During this period, we witnessed food arriving when we had none. No one knew we were struggling, money arriving in the mail when we had none left to cover bills, bags of free clothing appearing just as children had outgrown their own. One night, a drunk driver, who should have plunged into our bed through the wall behind us from the outside busy city road, miraculously went across the opposite lane into a shop window.

The Station Wagon

These were just a few wondrous signs of Heaven and Earth converging in synchronicity. One of the miracles we experienced regularly was from an unlikely source. It was our 'Yank Tank', a huge monstrosity of a station wagon my husband purchased at the time to carry our three little ones. Our children ranged from three months to four years of age, and their car seats all fit across the backseat. Despite the enormous petrol consumption of this car, at times it refused to take very much. It would stop pumping after only a few minutes, and, on checking, the tank was always full.

On two vivid occasions, we had left the noisy inner-city home to travel several hours into the countryside for a scenic change and enjoyment. On each occasion, we returned with over a good hour or two left, only to realise we were almost out of petrol and had no money. I would pray the entire way home, and each time we miraculously made it safely back. We knew beyond any doubt that God had intervened to help us. Synchronicity!

Ann's Father Passing

God has been teaching me on my spiritual journey to see each second as Sacred, to know He is always Present and to ask for eyes to 'see' and to be open. I have always known when my twin would call, was in pain, or needed encouragement. I have grown up aware of these sensations, and distance has not prevented this synchronicity. The day my father passed away in July 2011, I was just about to board a plane to travel to see him. He had not been doing well, and I knew it was time. The last time I had seen him was two years prior.

After I arrived in Sydney, I stayed with my Mum in her villa in preparation for the funeral service the following morning and the arrival of my older brother from Nebraska, USA. That evening I tucked Mum into bed and walked over to her bedroom window to admire the twinkling lights along the coastline that always brought her joy. As I stepped near the window, I experienced a beautiful, warm, moist, and relaxing envelopment of air. I assumed it was a heat duct in the ceiling, but to my surprise, there was no duct anywhere! Then I knew. It was my father saying hello and apologising for leaving before I had arrived to see him one last time.

Since then, and after my mother passed in 2017, I have encountered this beautiful air several times in my bedroom here in the USA.

Ann's Mother Passing

Often nature can be a sign of synchronicity. Once you know this, you can observe the spiritual message representative of each animal or bird. My mother declined quickly after a cancer prognosis. I flew down to Sydney, Australia, for a week to help put her into hospice and pack up her belongings from her beautiful villa in July 2017. There, I was blessed to pray with her numerous times. And to give her my blessing and thanks for her life and love. My husband and I were booked to return and spend December with our eldest son (who also lives in Sydney) to visit her daily. The call that she was dying and not going to last 48 hours was very difficult to hear later in October. We had our eldest daughter's wedding in less than two weeks. I was heartbroken not to be able to get there for my Mum.

Fig. 23: Ann's parents

The night she passed in Sydney, I awoke in Chicago to someone gently sweeping a strand of hair across my forehead. I knew it was my mother before I received the call from Australia confirming the news. Later that day, three sparrows alighted our bedroom window and sat there a long-time looking in. This had never happened before. My mother had experienced a stillbirth for her first child. The three birds represented my parents and my eldest sister. I grew up in a suburb of Sydney's north shore surrounded by nature and birdlife. On our large extended deck's railing, Kookaburras, parrots, and white cockatoos were a daily sight. It was no surprise these three birds appeared the day my mother crossed over. Nicola Tesla wrote:

"If you want to find the universe's secrets, think in terms of energy, frequency, and vibration."

Synchronicity teaches us to become consciously aware of these terms and the nature of numbers. 'Angel' numbers have become a recent discovery for me over the last few years. These number frequency patterns represent messages the universe sends for us to pay attention to how we are living our lives now. An example would be 11:11, which is a call to return to reflect on your life purpose, a return to balance and to realise a life lesson is in front of us. It is not about being obsessed with always watching the time or for these signs, but simply going about your day and realising it is a moment of synchronicity when you do notice a number pattern.

The veil between Heaven and Earth is very, very thin. Perhaps it does not even exist? I believe a new time is quickly approaching where we will 'see with new eyes, and Heaven will manifest before us. Our loved ones who have gone before us have never left our sides. Heaven and Earth will have eclipsed.

Kieran and Faye

In *Is Mise Cara,* we discuss the visits and presence of Cara on numerous occasions. As mentioned earlier, it was not just to immediate family. Cara appeared to the international businessman and now good family friend, Khalid Mukhtar (See chapter 'Khalid's Vision'). Khalid explains how Cara appeared to him and parted with a beautiful smile and a spiritual request. In another chapter, 'Girl With The Long Dark Hair' we describe another of these appearances. See the excerpt below:

"Faye lay restless in bed thinking about Cara and struggled to sleep. Turning and stretching out her hand, she touched what she felt was the back of Finn's head. After a few moments, Faye noticed how plush and soft the hair felt. Her hand continued past where Finn's short hair should have stopped, travelling past the neck before resting on the lower back area. Recognising the dark hair, she immediately sensed the close and immediate presence of Cara."

One morning, Faye's grandmother Margaret was seriously ill. Faye's aunt Patricia was en- route to Leeds from her home in Italy for a traditional summer visit when the event occurred. Faye's dad collected Patricia from Leeds Bradford Airport and hurried back to Margaret's home. The chance of Patricia flying that morning and getting some hours with Margaret before she passed that night seemed like meaningful synchronicity. Like she wanted all three children together one last time before departing.

St Margaret's York Shrine

Shortly before Cara passed, Faye had a similar experience to Ann's when visiting the little church of St Margaret's (Shrine of Saint Margaret Clitherow) in York, England. The *Is Mise Cara* book discusses how St Margaret was crushed to death for her Catholic faith. While praying, we wrote how:

"Faye felt a cold breeze drift past when praying at the front of the church. She quickly turned, surprised not to see Cara or Finn behind

her. They were standing at the back of the aisle alongside me. Faye believes that someone or something had crossed her path in that tiny church".

Cara then sat with her legs hanging over the small ledge at the back of the church and wrote something in the visitor book. We returned a year later to find that the church had been closed during the pandemic. Fortunately, we contacted the local priest, who emailed a picture of Cara's note. Cara had asked people to:

"Pray for the world, family, friends, and my future health".

Fig. 24 Cara and Finn at St Margaret's Shrine in York

Kieran at St Margaret's Shrine (Summer of 2022)

Rosie Walsh (Physic Medium from Kerry, Ireland) asked if we were mediums after viewing the pictures and videos captured since Cara passed. We certainly don't see ourselves as mediums but have no doubt that the spirits are frequently reaching out. We discussed another remarkable synchronicity in the summer of 2022 when visiting the same small chapel with Faye and Finn. We sensed the energy while praying, and spent about 15 minutes talking about Cara. Finn walked out so Faye followed, and quickly returned, holding the front door for me. As we debated where to go for a quick drink, I felt tingles run down the back of one leg. Like static. The Shrine was empty apart from us, so you can imagine how my heart skipped a beat when something gently grabbed the base of my leg. Looking straight at Faye, I began telling her what was happening when a second small hand appeared around the Achilles on my second leg. We just looked at each other, wondering what was going on around us. It seemed comforting but also absolute madness. We shared this with Lorna in our final meeting, who advised that this small space would have been filled with a significant body of spirits. And how this would have been the soul of a little child who was acknowledging our presence.

19

PENNIES FROM HEAVEN (BELFAST, IRELAND)

by Bridette Mawhinney

"It's only Skin". Skin was her nickname for Tomás. Seeing my shocked expression, she always told us, "It's not the dead you have to fear but the living".

Collette with daughters. Beloved mother of Michelle, Julieanne, Gerard, Marian, Bridette, and Rachel,

In October 2019, my mummy found out she had a tumour in her throat. Further tests later showed it was an aggressive Stage 4 Oesophageal Cancer spreading rapidly. Due to her age being 64, plus other medical complications, she decided she wouldn't survive surgery or radiation sessions. In December 2019 was given four-six months to live. My mummy was always highly spiritual. For instance, she said prayers for everyone, was an avid mass-goer, and lit candles for everything and everyone. Late January 2020, after sitting on her chair in the living room, she joined me at the window for a cigarette before remarking:

"I saw Tomás at the window; he was waving at me for a couple of minutes". Tomás passed away aged 16 in 2001 with a heart condition. I said to my mummy, "are you sure?" She then described how he was standing and

waving. My mummy had waved back before she looked again, and he had gone away. Now, she wasn't on any hard medication or treatment and was adamant about what she saw.

A few days later, she shared with my other sister and me that Tomás had revisited. This time, he came closer to her window and waved in. She wasn't ever scared of the vision or even her own health problems, even though my mummy knew it was a terminal condition.

Gradually, she described how many more visitors emerged from a different realm. She seemed very content with this and, in April 2020, passed at home. Her spiritual visitors brought calmness and eased any fears for her to die peacefully.

This event wasn't the first time she had heard from Tomas. In the house where we grew up, the old floorboards upstairs would creek when someone walked on them. On many occasions, while sitting in the living room, I would ask who was upstairs after hearing what sounded like people walking into the room and sitting on the bed. My mummy would say, "it's only Skin". Skin was her nickname for Tomás. Seeing my shocked expression, she always told us, "It's not the dead you have to fear but the living". However, like all mothers, my mummy wore a cloak of bravery. She made her arrangements and said what needed to be said. When I asked her how I would know she was true to me, she said I would leave you five pence pieces (5p coins) to collect. I remember laughing when she said this.

In April 2020, she left this realm for the next. The days, weeks and months followed. Every day my kids and I would find 5p's in random places, e.g., on their beds, in my kitchen, beside the kettle, in the car and at school.

A year later, my daddy passed suddenly in May 2021, and we are finding 5ps everywhere. So now I have the same little jar under my sink. My mummy also collected five pence pieces in a little jar under her kitchen sink. It became a novelty with her grandkids, which would help her fill it up but help her empty it just as quickly. Her initial terminal cancer diagnosis was earth-shattering for us all.

Kieran and Faye

Faye and I occasionally feel the presence of a child, which we believe to be Cara, in our bed. One March night, I looked up from my pillow and saw a child with what seemed like fair hair in bed between us. It seemed strange because Finn's hair was much darker now. I drifted to sleep then a while later, after returning from the bathroom during the night, I remember seeing the child, who I believed to be Finn, in a sound sleep. A while later, I snuggled into Faye and enquired about Finn's whereabouts. Faye said she also thought that Finn was in our bed earlier. Finn left his bed after hearing us talking and joined us as we lay there in the dark. He'd slept alone all night. To us, we are certain that it was Cara.

On another night in May, I asked Cara for a sign when drifting off to sleep and soon felt a strange tingling sensation in my hair. Lorna Byrne mentioned something similar when referring to the angels ruffling her hair (see 'Angels in my Hair'). Feeling cold symptoms in early June, I struggled to sleep. After awakening in the early hours, I lay planning my day – considering the charity registration process and the families we'd be able to help through a holiday home. Just then, I heard the unmistakable noise of a child running to our room, just like Finn would have done when younger. Sensing the bed move at my feet and assuming it was Finn, I turned and lifted the quilt to see Finn was already fast asleep between us. I lay back and said: 'hello there, Cara Mia'. Later, while still in the wee hours, I woke again to the feeling of someone sitting at my feet. Wondering if Finn had climbed out, I noticed he was asleep in the space between us. I sensed Cara's presence once again.
One late February morning in 2021, I slowly recited the Hail Mary in Irish,

remembering many beautiful moments with Cara. Around 6:30 am, I looked to my left to see Finn sleeping soundly, facing me but a few inches down the pillow and head pointed downwards - snugged between Faye and me. The room was bright enough to see the most striking image of a little girl's face, which seemed to merge into Finn's fair hair.

A thin but exquisite face – with a sharp chin and high cheekbones. About four years old, part of her face wedged into the pillow. A stunning blend of soft pale skin and jet-black hair – wavy and down to her eyebrows. Her eyes stood out; they didn't appear human. Like blood orange slits, they slowly opened, almost dilated, and closed every few seconds. The lips and mouth changed, too, as she appeared to blow little kisses into the pillow. I rubbed my eyes, then returned my gaze to where she lay and noticed Finn's hand slowly moving up his face and resting on the spot where the girl's face appeared. I rubbed my eyes again and wondered how mad this was and if I had imagined it.

I then closed my eyes, and upon reopening them, the little girl had turned her head and was now looking at me directly. We just lay and looked at each other for a while as I slowly recited a decade of the rosary – looking directly at what appeared to be Cara. The face also resembled many younger faces around her bedroom while the eyes were slowly opening and closing. The mouth area was changing in appearance. As I prayed, this beautiful little creature stared with alien-like eyes and smiled widely on several occasions before returning to her normal position.

I considered embracing her but remembered Lorna's words about 'leaving them to it'. They are on a unique journey. Ultra-pure and not to be approached. The whole experience lasted about 30 minutes before Finn woke. Heading straight for his mum, arms outstretched, then pulled me over for a hug. I asked him about his dream, curious to know if he'd had an experience. He mentioned Cara and her friends playing and one girl who previously caused some distress to

Cara. We then discussed the experience together over breakfast. We're fascinated to know how the reader would deal with these supernatural and paranormal experiences. They are mainly positive, or certainly seem so - but not always.

Figure akin to Our Lady

On another night, I awoke to a glow in the corner of our darkened bedroom. Below Cara's picture (site of the chapter 'Red Orbs are Circling') in *Is Mise Cara*, a small figure appeared. It was approximately three feet in height, akin to Our Lady. A sparkling halo glowed directly above. It resembled a fountain of water being sprayed from behind her head, stopping at her brow - continuously. With no other possible light sources, it seemed to be happening for a reason. I've seen countless physical statues and figures of Our Lady to realise it was identical. But why was it appearing beneath this location? Directly above is the site of a new large picture, replacing the previous picture that smashed to the floor after Cara's death as we slept during the early hours. A family picture of us praying at a shrine in Ardara in Donegal replaced it. When Faye awoke, she thought she'd heard a child running during the night.

Cara's Pendant

Faye was gifted a pendant from the Macmillan nursing team with Cara's fingerprint engraved, taken when Cara lay at rest in the morgue. One morning, the chain snapped, and the pendant seemed to have disappeared from where it dropped in the bedroom. She tore the room apart, trying to find it. The next day, Faye mentioned how she still couldn't locate Cara's pendant and continued looking around where it had dropped. She then discussed aloud, "Come on, Cara; help me find this pendant". At the same moment, I felt drawn to look across the room after noticing something glimmering on the carpet. I found the pendant literally as Faye spoke those words. Cara seems to have guided me.

Nana's Needle

Cara's Nana Hazel was in our garden, helping sew part of the canopy for sun cover. Somehow, she managed to drop a needle in the grass and searched high and low, worried that someone would walk on it. After quite a while of searching, she said, "Come on, Cara, where is it?" I happened to be strolling past when I heard Hazel. After asking what she'd lost, I was compelled to look in one area and noticed it immediately. We all laughed and thanked Cara because I was lost without my glasses and couldn't see more than a few feet in front of me. My mother's needle remains wedged in my foot from the 1980s in Belfast. As a result, I could not enter the MRI room with Cara during her brain scans because of the magnetic force of the MRI machines.

20

INEZ SYLVIA JOHNSON (JAMAICA)

by Rohan Johnson from Jamaica [based in Cork, Ireland]

"A moment in time, an event, crossing paths with that random stranger, losing a loved one, or experiencing a catastrophe. Such events could be a turning point that changes your life journey, your children, and your family's life for better or worse".

Fig. 26 Inez Johnson

INEZ SYLVIA JOHNSON (JAMAICA)

Coincidental or Meaningful Manifestations

It was late 2018, and as I reflected on the loss of my eldest sister and four of my closest friends, I felt deflated and beaten down. All at once, it appeared that most things were spiralling out of control. It was also when I had one of the most traumatic experiences, having been physically attacked in my home by a random stranger. In time, this experience would alter the course of my journey through life.

Suddenly I was in a state of limbo. Nevertheless, a greater part of me realised that I had a responsibility to my beloved mother and those who were dear to me. Months later, I surrendered to accepting the bitter truth that I had little or no control over anything other than how I prepared myself to handle these situations. Were cosmic energies at play, or was it the hand I was dealt here and now? I pondered; how could I make the most of these bad experiences? But, unable to make sense of it all, I found myself perpetually obsessed with understanding the special significance of these connections of events and their underlying oneness.

I was now at a point where I needed help to determine what was missing. I had a burning desire to understand better life's coincidental events. It set me on a spiritual path, one of self-negotiation and self-discovery. In truth, it was a challenge to fully comprehend the causes and manner in which things occurred in our everyday lives. And how certain events seemed to manifest themselves in a well-organised but complex pattern. In time, I embraced my imperfections and acknowledged that these coincidental events were strongly related and a large part of life's grander scheme. It was time to find a new path.

It began with mindfulness, becoming aware of what was happening around me and developing an attitude of acceptance of where I found myself. Things became more apparent within months after entering the new year, 2019. I decided to try meditation which, undoubtedly, I struggled with at first. Let's say I was a man who had no time for himself, let alone to allow for time to quiet the mind.

In my quest to understand the meaning of things, I came across Dr Wayne Dwyer's (an American self-help author and a motivational speaker) "101 Ways to Transform Your Life". He opines that one should "Forgive yourself for your transgressions". "See that mistakes are lessons for you to transcend". He postulated "that there are no accidents in our intelligent universe, and one should realise that everything that shows up in your life has something to teach you". Admittedly, I was sceptical but very intrigued by his creative process of compiling such a masterful piece of work. Still, I was drawn to what I believe was one of his most life-altering quotes as follows:

"If you change the way you look at things, the things you look at change".

His work has profoundly influenced me through self-transformation, and spiritual development, which led me to engage in practising the art of mindfulness and meditation. These tools would become instrumental as my mettle was about to be tested when I lost my love: my dear mother, role model and Queen.

I recalled it was Thursday, 10th June 2021, when I rang my mother. She answered the phone and sounded ok but somewhat not her usual self. We chatted for a few minutes, and I told her I was about to start a new job the following day. However, I was still unsure if I was making the right decisions and needed her wisdom. But as the old saying goes, mothers know best, and in her reply, she said, "my son, follow your heart just as we discussed before".

She reiterated, "your spirit will guide you", and I ended the call shortly afterwards. However, deep inside, I had this strange feeling that one can't explain. I wanted to tell her that whatever was happening, she needed to stick around to see the completion of the two projects I was working on. One of which she often says she wants to live long enough to read my work. To this day, I don't know what prevented me from sending my mother that message.

It was now Friday, 11th June. It was a beautiful day. It was the perfect weather for capturing stunning photographs, and I wouldn't miss that opportunity. So, I grabbed my camera equipment and headed towards Charles Fort, Summercove, Kinsale, County Cork, Ireland, approximately a 31-minute drive from my home. As surreal as it was, everything felt wonderfully perfect capturing mother nature at her best. My only shortcoming was the need for more time to bask in the awesome splendour and be in nature's beautiful surroundings.

For the first time in a long time, I felt truly liberated, at ease and better understood my purpose and the meaning of life. I was in a state of "being" and feeling overwhelmed with gratitude. The flowers, the sounds of the ocean and the clear blue skies brought me into a state of appreciation. And also, an awareness that I was a very fortunate man to be part of this marvelous creation. Little did I know that everything that occurred up to that moment prepared me for what was yet to come.

In the blink of an eye, the moments quickly passed. It was about 2:30 pm, and it was time to head home and prepare for work at 5 pm that same day, so there was no real urgency to rush home. Approximately 20 minutes into my journey, I got caught up in traffic that appeared to be at a standstill. I had no concerns because I had plenty of time, was familiar with the surrounding areas, and knew some alternate routes. On reflection, each moment spent sitting in the traffic went from minutes to an hour. Every alternate route was becoming a roadblock.

At around or sometime after 3:30 pm, I got a call from one of my childhood friends in Canada. I told him I had a strange feeling about my mother not being her usual self and wanted to ask her to hang around a little longer because I needed her to be here to see my work. I remember mentioning that

I didn't get a sense that mom was in a state of transition. I also remember whining about the traffic jam that seems to be the "traffic jam from hell" because I have lived in the City of Cork for several years now. Still, I don't recall ever seeing such a traffic jam.

I began to feel anxious and panicked about the situation. I started to question the whole meaning of what was happening. My beautiful day was becoming a nightmare, and the feeling of ecstasy was rapidly fading away.

After waiting around in the traffic for what seemed to be an eternity, I was now home with little or no time to shower and prepare for work. I quickly got dressed and headed for work. It was now 4:35 pm, and I would have to face this traffic dilemma again. At roughly 4:50 pm, I called my manager to explain the traffic situation. Luckily for me, he was fully aware of what was happening around the city and suburbs.

At 4:55 pm, my phone rang. It was my sister, Elizabeth. Her voice trembles as she tries to hold back her tears and emotions. She said, "Brother, mom has gone".

Then for a moment, there was a deafening silence. Time stood still. Your mind goes blank, and suddenly we are both lost for words. For a few minutes, we consoled each other, but at that moment, we were powerless. I remember thinking our most dreaded fear had manifested itself, and there was still nothing we could do.

Finally, it was our time to experience the most "painful pain". Our love for mother was indescribable and to lose her was something we never imagined we could genuinely handle. For reasons unknown, coincidental events or unforgiving happenings can play a pivotal role in human transformation. They can have an adverse effect, providing that soft cushion to cope with anything that comes our way.

Dr Wayne Dwyer suggests that: only when we "accept that there are no accidents in our intelligent universe and realise that everything that shows up in our life has something to teach us" could we begin to function with a higher state of consciousness. Thus, it becomes essential to develop a keen self-awareness and acknowledge that all things are intertwined and that nothing in existence is separate or occurs as an unbroken entity.

In the end, these coincidental or meaningful manifestations could serve as crucial mechanisms to support our journey to new self-transformation, self-discovery, and self-awareness and bring us in unity with "self" and all things in existence.

Rohan's story overlaps with the following chapter written by Charles Stevens.

21

AN UNEXPLAINED COINCIDENCE (PAPUA NEW GUINEA)

by Charles Stevens

AN UNEXPLAINED COINCIDENCE (PAPUA NEW GUINEA)

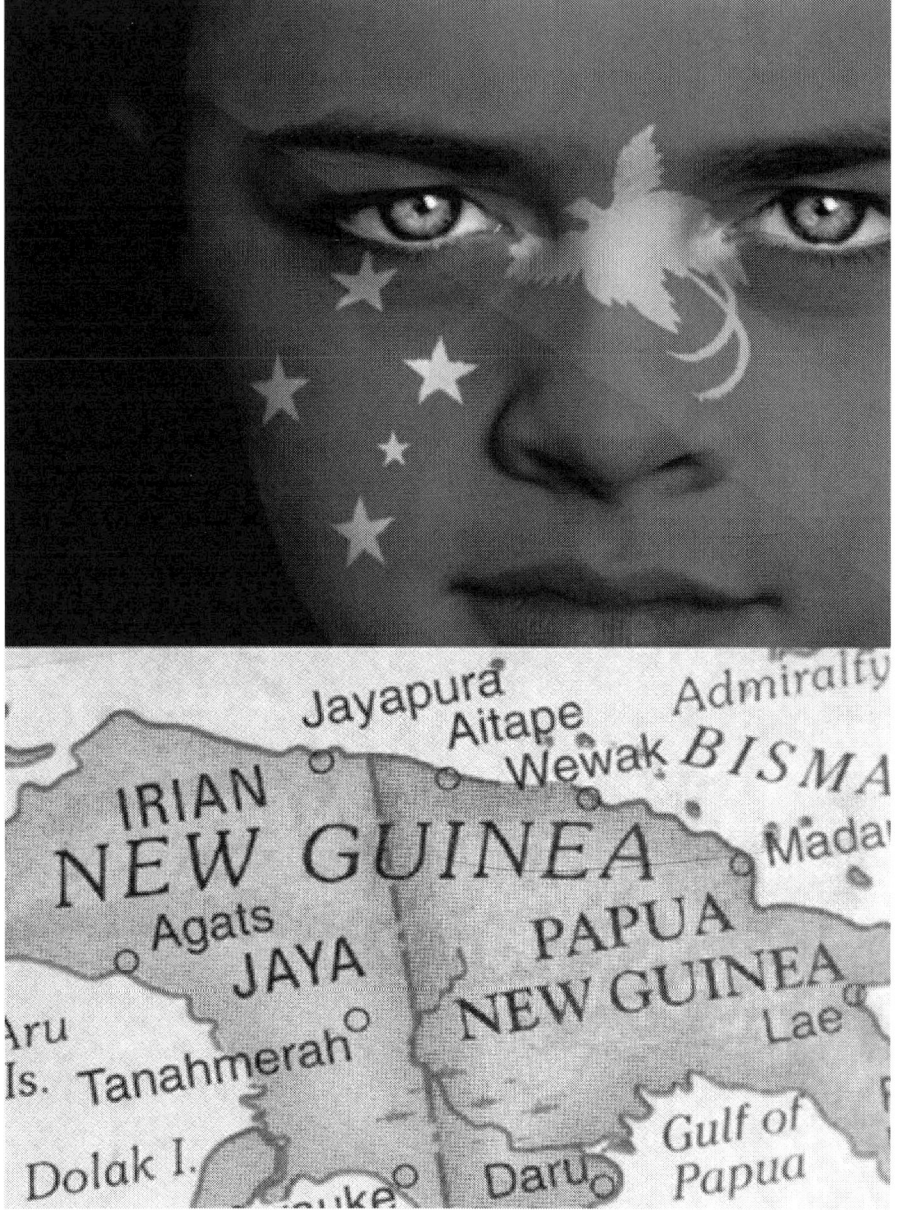

Fig 27 Source: Canva Pro

Shortly after leaving school in 1964, at the age of 19, I returned home to become a volunteer with Voluntary Service Overseas (VSO). I went to Papua New Guinea to work as a teacher in an Anglican Mission Primary school. I was the teacher for the top class, all of whom were expected to proceed on to either practical training or formal secondary education.

The student's age ranges were between 14 and 25 years of age. I also had other duties, such as managing the Mission Shop, which brought me into contact with the local villagers. Occasionally, I would visit those villages.

One of the village elders was a very remarkable man called Elijah. He would visit the school occasionally, sit down with the pupils, and tell them stories about World War 2. He'd discuss what happened when the Japanese invaded the local area and when the American troops later came.

He was revered by the local tribes and hugely respected by all of us at the Mission. The Mission also had a hospital and a leper colony; we often donated blood when needed. Still, the local villagers believed that giving blood was to transfer your spirit to the person receiving the blood. Consequently, there was real fear and serious resistance to blood donation. Despite this, Elijah became the first local person to give blood. It was a remarkable act of courage on his part.

One day I was taking a class at school when, at around 9am, we noticed a stretcher bringing someone to the hospital and the word went about that it was Elijah. I thought nothing of it as it was a fairly regular occurrence. The class went on as normal until about an hour later when one of the girls in the class became suddenly hysterical and uncontrollable.

I had to arrange for her to return home. At least an hour after this there was great wailing coming from the hospital and we learned that Elijah had died. It was only then that the students told me that Elijah was the girl's grandfather.

AN UNEXPLAINED COINCIDENCE (PAPUA NEW GUINEA)

Somehow, she had two hours of advanced notice of her grandfather's death. I was astounded! Despite the circumstances, there had to have been some form of spiritual communication between them to understand the reaction I had witnessed. I believed this to have happened at the time, and I still think about it today.

Although I acknowledge that there may well be explanations that we discover in the future, my conclusions then and now are threefold:

1. In certain circumstances, spiritual communication is indeed possible.
2. There are areas of human experience about which we know and understand very little.
3. There are areas of human sensitivity which we in the modern world have lost.

Indeed, I believe that our modern world has suppressed such sensitivity by way of the manner of our development and expectations

In today's world, our reaction can be sceptical, or shocked and a little frightened when we come across and have personal experience of these kinds of spiritual occurrences. We need to accept that we don't yet have all the answers in our materialistic and scientifically based existence.

22

THE LETTER ~ DEBBIE LAMOUR (IRELAND)

b y Jack Lamour in memory of his wife, Debbie

"The fact that Debbie had found a person who lived so close to Kate. And how this particular girl was so open to a spirit from the sacred realm contacting her while deep in meditation qualifies it as a meaningful synchronicity".

Fig. 28 Debbie Lamour (RIP)

Kate and her family live deep in the Dromara countryside. The area they live in is really isolated - there are only a few houses and a small church in it. One of the nearby buildings was, at that time, being used as a religious retreat/women's centre by various groups, including Buddhists.

A few months after Debbie died, a woman called to Kate's house (literally just a stone's throw from the center) and, after introducing herself, asked Kate if she had a recent family bereavement. Kate told the girl her sister, Debbie, had recently died.

The girl handed Kate a letter, told her very briefly what had happened to her, asked Kate to read it, and then walked back to the centre.

In the letter, she said she followed Buddhism. During one of her meditation sessions, she was acutely aware of another presence in the room with her. She said she could hear a voice faintly at first, but becoming clearer, and the (female) voice identified itself as my late wife, Debbie Larmour.

The voice asked the girl if she would write down a message and deliver it to Debbie's sister, who, as I said, lived close by. The girl said the voice was insistent that she should write it down on a piece of paper and give it to Kate. The girl agreed to do it.

Eventually, Debbie asked her to tell Kate [and the family] not to worry about her; she was fine and happy and no longer affected by her disability. She didn't want anyone to be sad because of her passing, wanting them all to be happy and go on with their lives. She also mentioned a few other people and our nieces and nephews.

She then told Kate about a necklace and charm that had something to do with a horse. Kate didn't quite understand what that meant at the time; whether Debbie wanted her to look for such a necklace, or what relevance it had to her.

[Faye] I told you that I've been trying to find the letter that was given to me by Debbie's sister, Kate, after Debbie died. Unfortunately, I hadn't been able to find it after searching every likely place it could be in the house. Then, just as I was about to finish, the very last place I looked - a drawer in a dresser in my hall - in the last few pieces of paper I was going through before giving up, I lifted a piece of card with something handwritten on it.

It was a thank-you note from our niece, Indigo, thanking Debbie and me for the necklace and horse charm we had given her for a Christmas present. To be honest, I can't even remember getting such a card. It had probably been lying in the drawer for years, but the fact it was so relevant to the story makes it more than a mere coincidence, in my opinion.

Also, the fact that Debbie had found a person who lived so close to Kate, and that this particular girl was so open a spirit from the sacred realm contacting her while she was deep in meditation certainly, in my opinion, qualifies it as a meaningful synchronicity.

Attached is a photo of the note Jack's niece sent re: the necklace.

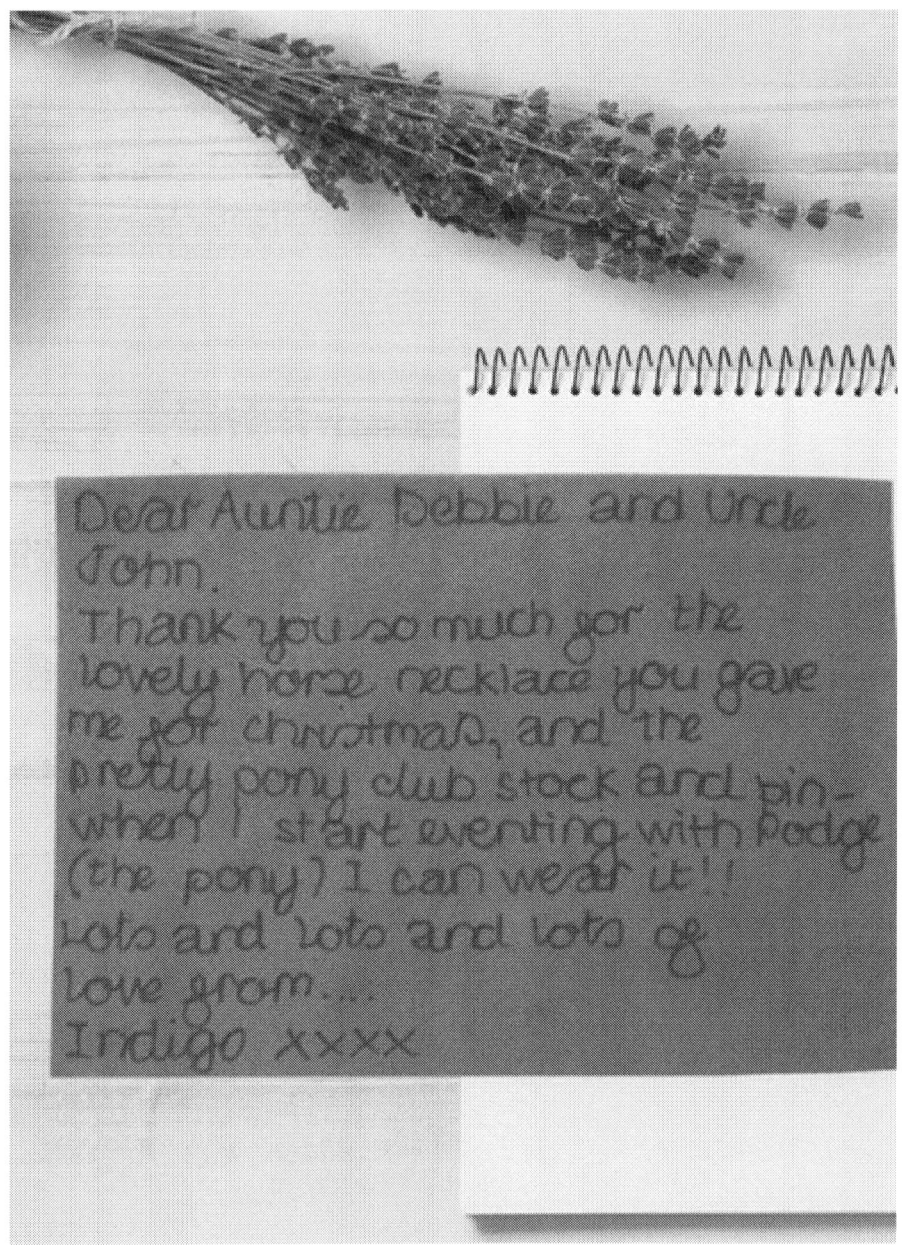

Fig. 29. The Letter

23

FLEUR ALANA & OTHERS (AUSTRALIA)

by Jacqueline (Jack) Hiddlestone-Mumford in Australia

"Since we lost Fleur, as each family member has passed, we have experienced something similar, which freaks some out, but I find it comforting. They are letting us know they are ok".

My elder sister (Joanne) passed in 2002 and mum (Jill – a neural phycologist who passed from breast cancer that moved to the brain) in 2008, so I keep these things to myself other than the occasional discussion with Muz or a discussion around the bedroom door opening and closing as a grown-up event we occasionally discuss at family gatherings.

Some say imagination, others spiritual beings, and others say it is just plain weird. Whatever slant, label or offering you want to put on it, these are the experiences I have had and, in some instances, those around and close to me have had with those that have passed. Some can't be explained no matter how much you try; others very much align to who the person was. Their energy remains for a reason.

As always, there are those everyday happenings that we all experience.

Things that just are! Perhaps it is like looking at a gift that simultaneously triggers a call from the person and contacting someone out of the blue who invariably needs your help or a chat because they are depressed. Or sensing when a sibling or parent is unwell even though they may be in a different state or country. For instance, I knew when to ring to check in or get someone checked on; thinking about a person you haven't spoken to for some time, and they ring you; it's those type of everyday happenings. In the following sections, I discuss the more unusual things that trigger an awareness, a wonder, without explanation.

I'm not religious, believing we drive our own destiny through the decisions we make, not some 'higher being'; and that our energy continues in some form after we pass, leaving our physical body. Although there are times where I do resolve, something happened because it is meant to be. Not being religious, however, doesn't mean I don't apply the fundamental basics we should all apply, nor dismiss others who want to explore or believe whatever religion/s they wish.

The fundamental basics include:

- *Showing respect and caring for others; supporting each other in our respective endeavours.*
- *Being truthful and ethical in everything we do; abiding by the laws that govern our world/country/community.*
- *Treating everyone as an equal (after all, we all breathe the same air; there is no place for racism, ageism, sexism, classism and all the other isms that are bandied around to insinuate someone is of higher standing or more deserving than another), to name but a few.*

I enjoy mentoring, supporting and guiding others to develop their capabilities to contribute to society. From doctoral cohort members moving through their module and thesis stage into post-Doctoral roles; Master and Undergraduate students in understanding and applying what they have learnt; people looking to get into or move through management and board roles in organisations; developing skills needed for work functions; or primary and high school students in learning how to learn to set their future from a sound base.

These drivers expand to volunteering in other areas as well. For instance, helping elders understand their options around anything from budgeting to aged care facilities and at-home services so they can decide how to best support their future needs. It may include providing meals; working with Indigenous students who experientially learn over rope learning that many schools expect; and community-based events such as leading teams of volunteer helpers at the Easter Show, community welcoming to tourists, and charities who cater for the wishes of sick kids, etc.

Enough of my current stance. The following is a collection of some of the experiences that have influenced who I have become and may give some insights into how some people evolve through their experiences and beliefs.

Family

We moved into an early 1900's house in the 1970's. Different configurations of siblings resided in the second bedroom over the years we were there as a family. It was one with cherubs in the sculptured ceiling. Our ages ranged from around 5 to 14. Every night at 9.00pm on the dot, the bedroom door opened and closed as if the occupants were being checked on. We couldn't explain this. No matter how many attempts we made of someone walking past to the bathroom or into the dining room, jumping, pushing the closed door, and the like; it didn't replicate.

We thought it was mum or dad, but neither had. Both claimed it wasn't them, they had been nowhere near the room at the time. This continued, lessening somewhat as the family moved out, heading in different directions, but stopped when we added an enclosed room under the house some years later, in the mid-1990's. The house feels different now.

These daily events continued to be a point of discussion at family gatherings. Different family members had heard or saw the door open and close, but no one seemed to be there. We called it 'our friendly ghost.' Some of the younger generation laugh at us, others relive their unexplained experiences in the house.

'The Others'

For those who know Australia and have travelled the main roads in Queensland, there is a section of highway in central Queensland between Mackay and Townsville which is notorious for accidents they would know well. Numerous signs tell us to be careful, it seems more so than on other sections of the highways.

I used to travel through there, usually between midnight and 2am by the time I reached that section. It gave you an unexplainably horrible yet eerily peaceful feeling along the entire section of road, keeping you alert and awake. I felt I could see people at the side of the road, different ages, different attire, some standing, some sitting, an old car, a cart and horse. At times it caught you off guard, fleetingly in the headlights, then appear as solid as they come, some on the edge of the road, others further back. It got to the stage where I knew what was coming up next for the most part.

One day, I was sure a car had had an accident, strewn across the road in front of me. I stopped to see if I could lend a hand. Getting out of the car, I grabbed my first aid kit, a blanket and torch and moved towards the wreckage. As I approached, a young girl in her 20s sitting in the driver's seat raised her bloodied hand towards me and I watched her fade away. The car too, leaving only a scattering of small pieces of glass and oily sand left behind after sweeping up after an accident.

As I stood there, I felt stupid, what had I experienced? The accident had clearly been cleaned up, yet I saw the tangled wreck and the girl raising her hand, seeking help. I returned to my car and continued driving north. The next day's newspaper spoke about another young life lost on the notorious section of road. I had passed through the areas hours after the accident had been cleared and the road opened again. She was there again when I drove back south, appearing to the side of the road, raising her hand towards me as I passed by. Less visible this time.

Mum said she saw the same sort of thing and it was people that had passed along the road over the years. Some of my siblings told me I was crazy and just imagining it because I was driving tired and alone and shut the conversation down. The exception being my eldest sister who considered Fleur an old soul and my other siblings' younger souls who didn't understand.

On another occasion, my baby brother one day swore he saw an oncoming car on a bridge, swerving to miss a head-on accident and running down an embankment. When he got out of the car, there was no-one around, no sign of any other car. The same bridge had had a head-on recently. He then 'got' what I saw and didn't shut the associated conversation down so quickly.

'Our' Fleur Alana

Fleur Alana came to us in May 1980. The only sign of a possible problem was two fingers being webbed together, something that could be addressed as her hand grew. But it was a sign of what was to come. Her breathing laboured, and frequent trips to the hospital and specialists, etc, found her trachea was less than 1mm wide, and she was going to slowly choke unless it grew or medical intervention occurred. Months were spent in the Camperdown Children's Hospital, Goulburn and Canberra Hospitals. Fleur spent hour after hour in an oxygen tent, helping her to breathe. The wheeze ranges from mild to extremely laboured. The occasional break saw the family together in different locations, enjoying time outside the hospital environment and trying to make Fleur's time somewhat 'normal'.

Fig. 30 Dad with Fleur in 1981, sitting outside his pigeon ducket on one of the few days she was well enough to be out of hospital

With Fleur's trachea less than 1mm wide, she was slowly choking, her breathing was deteriorating, and she had virtually lived in her oxygen tent. The specialists looked at ways that could give her a fighting chance at a normal life. They searched locally and internationally for medical research. They recommended taking some muscle from near the heart and grafting it into the trachea; it would be the first operation of its kind in Australia. The operation was scheduled for a week later, a day after Joanne's 21st birthday. They operated and placed her into an induced coma so she would not move.

The nurses were brilliant, helping to care for her. But, on the 26th July 1981, that slight movement of the tube, was it Fleur waking slightly, a gag reflex, a slight turn not quite right? Something went horribly wrong, the tube moved and had to be carefully manoeuvred back into place, Fleur was choking, there was limited time to get the specialist back in, the medical staff did their best with what was facing them. We lost our precious Fleur that day, the family had changed forever.

We had lost siblings before it was their time to breathe, but this was different. Seeing that little white coffin is something no parent, sibling, aunt, uncle, grandparent, or cousin ever want to see. Dad found it hard, he said you shouldn't be burying your children and certainly not your grandchildren. He was right, of course.

The specialist asked if it was possible to do an autopsy to find out what went wrong and learn from it. It was up to the family to decide, and no pressure. To help no one ever go through the same, approval was given, and they said they were as careful as they could possibly be on her little body and learnt a lot. We had lost our Fleur Alana at just 14 months of age; she had spent most of her short life in hospitals. She didn't have time to grow, experience the wider world, yet made such an impression on the whole family.

Since Fleur's passing, we have had a presence in the occasional photo; some subtle, others quite blatant. Even using different cameras, it has continued, so it wasn't a specific camera. Quite often the shadows, unusual light placement and faded images show up, or an unusual instantaneous breeze in an enclosed room when we've been talking about Fleur, or when I've visited the family plot.

Setting up a Family Burial Plot

We all hear of a family member, just before passing, talking about someone who passed before them being with them. My grandfather referred to his armed forces comrade at the end of the bed, telling him it was ok. Nanna found this hard, but as always, supporting him through.

When we were looking to ensure Nanna could be buried next to Pop, we walked around the area to head over to his placement. Nanna stopped a few feet short and said, "they've turned their backs on me", visibly shaking. We moved away and looked for somewhere better suited for her. She found a nice family plot with a sun dial and views. When she got to the spot, she said, "Curl said here," and pointed to it. We checked, and yes, it was available. We purchased it and arranged for Pop to be relocated, ready for Nanna to join him sometime in the future. Nanna selected the inscription and plaque; Joanne selected the flat red granite base and an upright dual one for Fleur to be added to the same plot. It became the Hiddlestone Family Garden, with roses planted as well.

The Family Garden has seen additions since that time. Nanna, Joanne, Mum (Jill), and Dad (Jack) have all passed. Nanna has joined Pop in 2004, Joanne joined Fleur in 2002, and Dad in 2005 then Mum in 2008 joined them as well. Strangely, it can be totally out of season and an occasional single rose will bloom nearing a key milestone, be it a birthday, death, or anniversary. It's been the apricot rose bush nearest Fleur rather than the red rose bush that blooms out of season. I've spoken to the gardener there and he can't explain it. There is a sea of green and headstones/plaques across the cemetery and then this single apricot rose. If you weren't aware, it was there, you'd miss it.

Strange Happenings

In the period between Fleur's death in 1981 and Joanne's in 2002, she looked at alternate ways to address her diabetes and how it was ravaging her body. She and I went to a Mind, Body, Spirit event. We sat in on a white witch spell casting and talk, crystal bowl music, a clairvoyant, Indigenous healing, charka photo, image drawing and tarot reading. It was some event with a touch of everything to explore. Having an open mind to the event allowed for greater awareness of what is around us.

Three things stood out:

1. The charka photo of Joanne showed where she was ill, being black or washed out compared to the brighter colours elsewhere. The discussion with it told her she needed to seek medical attention in several areas.
2. The image drawing was her with Fleur somewhat faded in the background, as though watching from a distance. The guy said he could see this child image, just not quite detailed and that it was something he saw rarely, yet the drawing was uncannily like Fleur. We hadn't mentioned a child, only the interest in his pictures and wanted one done.
3. The third was the clairvoyant talk to a group. During the session, she looked directly at me and asked, "who is Kay? She wants to say thank you". Kay was three years old when she passed and is buried with Matthew, her cousin, who was ten months old. They are Mum's cousins. Mum had said she had a cousin buried in the same cemetery as her parents and grandmother. I went looking one day and found it overgrown with a whole tree/bush and broken parts. Not good

enough, I cleaned it up, repaired and added flowers whenever I visited family there. No other family member has visited, so I arranged for guardianship of the burial site to transfer to me along with the grandparents' site. This arrangement enabled me to maintain it without being questioned and advised if there were any issues to address. I assume this is who the clairvoyant is referring to. Then she turned to Joanne and told her Fleur was OK and watching over her until they were together again and that another child, a son, was to come, one that would make his mark.

At the end of the session, the clairvoyant asked Joanne to write a chapter for a book for her, something she didn't get the opportunity to do before she passed. Jo (Joanne) had the view that Fleur was an old soul, one that had gone through life's journey many times, knowing so much more beyond her tender 14 months and communicating without words.

Indeed, a boy did come. With Jo in a diabetic coma, at just 28 ½ weeks gestation, Murrie (our Muz) was born. A tiny 'cashew', as Dad called him, for the way he curled up. His entire body could sit in John's, my next brother down, hand. John is 6' 7", so he does have large hands. Muz spent the first months of his life in hospital in a humidly-crib, was this going to be a repeat of Fleur? Muz never got to meet his sister other than at her grave site. He fought and won. We were told had he been born a few days earlier, he would have had a cleft pallet, and it would remain thin throughout his life.

His main health complaints were frequent chest infections until his early twenties. He also experienced a level of sleep apnoea and was forced to wait an extra two years to play rugby as his spine wasn't strong enough. He has certainly worked hard and made his mark. Muz is multi-talented. He attended various Indigenous medicine, science and health-related camps that culminated in his chosen degree. He was also the first Indigenous Boarding Captain at his school. He explored combining bush medicine with allied health. Muz also undertakes an Indigenous Naming role; and is looking to preserve Indigenous languages, bush medicine and artefacts… to name a few. He is young, in his 20's and will make his mark. He was also a sports director at university; and is a confident public speaker who engages the audience and a budding actor.

We're not religious as such but Muz was brought up to explore and understand all religious views to better understand people, as well as why and how they think the way they do. It has served him well. He understands the (Indigenous) dreaming time and how that created or contributed to his world. Understanding some of the unknowns from other's perspectives may add further depth for him. There were times when Muz was young that he'd talk to someone we couldn't see.

This jokingly became Mr Nobody, but there were numerous discussions and laughter; it certainly wasn't Mr Nobody, it was very real to him, and he knew things that we hadn't spoken about or was on TV or in books he had read to him or read himself. It was though he was being educated on the ways of life; things he'd need to evolve as he got older.

The presence was a calming energy in the room. Muz didn't say who it was, but just gave me that look when I asked who he was talking to… the "really? Come on!" look he gives at times. So, I'd leave him to it and head off to do other things.

On other occasions when we spoke about family and in the occasional photo there is a shadowy image, a cool breeze crosses the room when all windows are closed, you feel a shove as though someone is laughing with you, or a knowing hand on the shoulder. These are normal; there is nothing to be scared about, accepting that it just is. At other times it is energy; a light floating that continues even when you block the sun or ceiling light from it to make sure it isn't a reflection of something bright; a face in clouds, or around the house.

Even this chapter was unusual. After writing 6,000 words, I saved it and put it aside to work on other documents with the intention to go back and finish. But when I looked for it, it was nowhere to be found... only a very early version. When rewriting one section, the computer kept shutting down for no reason, so I am taking that as some things are best left unsaid.

After Jo passed, Bill, Fleur's dad, visited. I gave him the camera they used to take so many photos over the years, particularly through the various Indigenous communities, along with the pictures that resonated with him. That night, as I lay in bed, no windows open, no reason for it, I felt a fleetingly strong cold wind across the room and a push, almost shove. I don't know if it is a positive acknowledgement that I did the right thing or a "why did you do that?' I take it as a positive acknowledgement that the camera and photos are with who they should be with. It's his connection to their past life and way of remembering the good times.

Since we lost Fleur, as each family member has passed, we've experienced something similar, which freaks some out, but I find it comforting. They're letting us know they are OK.

Faye and Kieran

Cara and Fleur's stories have much in common. While shopping at a supermarket in Leeds, a Thai lady on the tills often remarked how Cara was wise beyond her years. How being born so early put her in a special realm. One evening in Cara's room, I recorded some flickering lights and white mist on my phone. For the second time in recent weeks, I spotted a male figure. It appeared to be a man of substance, and what Faye, I and many others wonder if it's the Lord, God himself. I flicked some holy water around the site of the appearance and said a quick prayer.

The video in question is available in the *Is Mise Cara* YouTube

account. These 'visitations' often occur in real time. Faye immediately mentioned its resemblance to the holy picture of God in my mothers' hallway in Ireland. Later that evening, a stream of text messages arrived from my family in Ireland and colleagues in Nigeria. All agreed that the image appeared to be an extremely holy figure, perhaps Jesus Christ himself.

Early next morning we lay in bed, reminiscing about Cara and how she loved preparing for and celebrating Mother's Day with Faye. Finn brought the Mother's Day presents and after some laughs, tears and hugs I brought Faye a cup of tea and chocolates sent by a kind woman from Surrey. After 11 am mass, we visited Bradford for lunch, before driving home to watch the Manchester United match. After celebrating Mother's Day with a meal in Horsforth, we returned home and visited Cara's room. I sensed the energy before noticing the white mist rising slowly from the corner of the bed. I knew Cara was around.

The next morning, I flicked through the pictures and immediately noticed the face of a young child with what appeared to be a pink cloak around its head (See Figures 10 and 11). After sharing with family and friends, my phone began to buzz with WhatsApp messages. Almost everyone spotted the little face with a hood and cloak. We were also startled by other faces that emerged around the confines of the picture. These appeared to be a combination of older souls and babies, alongside an angel-like figure in the centre picture. These types of events continue unabated, and we still often wonder what the messages entail.

My cousin Bridette from Belfast believes that Cara's room is a portal for young souls. Maybe Cara somehow acts as a conduit for souls between the physical and spiritual worlds? In the next story, we discuss some of Cara's premonitions.

24

CARA'S PREMONITIONS (IRELAND/LEEDS)

Why is the man lying on top of a motorbike at the bottom of your bed'?

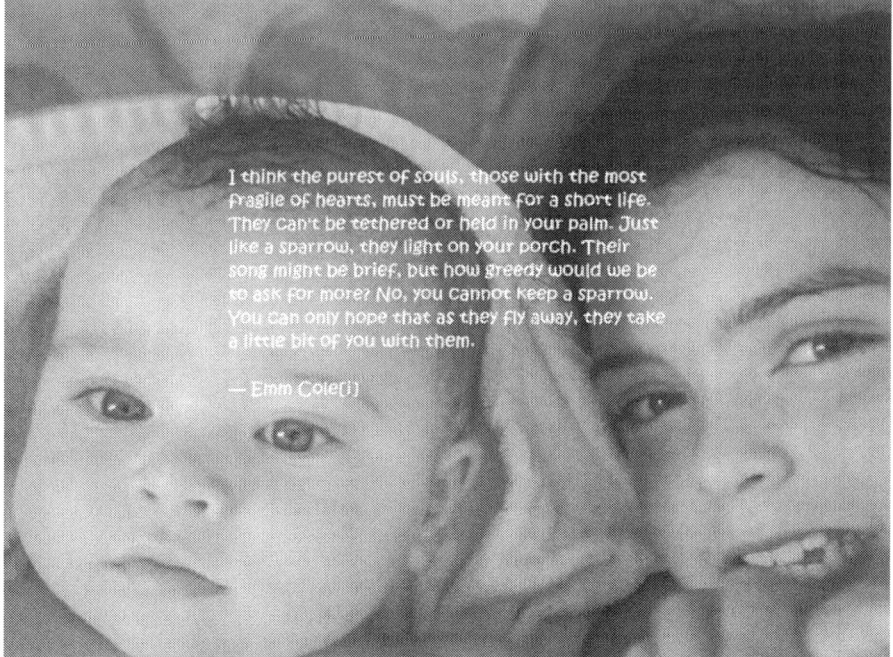

Fig. 31 Cara and Finn

In *Is Mise Cara*, we discuss how Cara had shared visions and dreams about bereavement and the afterlife before she passed. When we lived in Bramley, Leeds, a close relative and his partner were killed in a motorbike accident. Such a devastating loss – especially for his young family, sisters, and parents. After the accident, Cara strolled into our bedroom and asked: *"Why is there a man lying on top of a motorbike at the bottom of your bed?"* Months later, she remarked about seeing the man on the motorbike lying on the floor a second time. When Cara died, we went through her school notes and found a message about Christmas 2019 and how she'd imagined that Jesus would say to her:

"Make the most of Christmas 2019 with your family."

Below is another of Cara's stories written two months before she passed, about a: 'haunted house'.

CARA'S PREMONITIONS (IRELAND/LEEDS)

Story by Cara Mervyn – Aged 11.

This story is about a girl who lost he mother at a young age. Over the years strange things started happened and then finally she finds a box from her mother with a special gift inside...

It all began on the 13th October 1994, and the Smiths family were very busy as it was their daughters (Emily`s) 7th birthday the next day. Only this would be the last birthday they spent together. It was the 14th of October and Emily's birthday. She rushed downstairs waking up her parents "It's my birthday, it's my birthday" she exclaimed. She walked into the living room and her eyes opened wide as she looked down at all the presents on the floor. Mr and Mrs Smith walked through the door "Happy Birthday Darling!" they said, as they both passed Emily her presents. "Thank you!" said Emily with a huge smile on her face, though her mum didn't look happy, but Emily took no notice. Later on, they went for a meal to celebrate Emily's birthday. A few days later the mother passed away and Emily was devastated, but this was only the start of the strange things that were about to happen.

Strange things started happening around the house shortly after the funeral when Emily returned home with her father. She noticed that the tv would oddly turn off by itself and a window would often fly open unexpectedly. Her dad also noticed these strange things happening like his car keys were being misplaced and the bed would unmake itself once you waked out of the room. Once when Emily and her Dad were talking in the bedroom, they were shocked to hear a voice sounding just like her mum, shouting, "Dinners ready!" They were both white as a ghost as they waked downstairs and to their disbelief, dinner was served at the table but their mothers plate and cup was empty... Years later, Emily had a dream about a silver jewellery box with sparkling rings and diamonds. In her dream, she walked to the desk, trembling and unsure who had placed it there. She gazed at the small mirror on the jewellery box, and jumped when she seen the face smiling back at her. It was her mother. Her mother spoke gently and told her not to be afraid. She told her that this box was a special present that she had meant to give her for her 7th birthday, and she should take very good care not to lose it. Emily's eyes filed with tears of sadness but also joy at seeing her mother again. She reached out to touch the mirror when suddenly a voice called. It was her Dad calling her for breakfast. Her heart was pumping and she slowly opened her eyes and realised it was all a dream...

25

THE CLOCK (MADAGASCAR)

by Harigo Andre (Madigascar)

In memories of my late father, Bernard Randriamampianina
9 September 1934 – 9 September 2022

THE CLOCK (MADAGASCAR)

Fig. 32 Harigo's Dad

It was a beautiful Sunday morning on 22nd August 2004 in Antananarivo, the capital city of Madagascar, a few hours before I embarked on a trip to join my brother Eric in Mahajanga. This place is situated in the far east coast of the island, six hundred kilometers away from the capital. There were three of us at home in the lounge; dad, me and my nephew Brice. Around 9.30 am30am right after we watched some television, I rushed for a shower before preparing to take a taxi to the main bus station for the Mahajanga trip. Brice knocked at the bathroom door, hyperventilating, and screamed: "Hey uncle, uncle please come out quickly, something has happened to Grandpa".

After entering the room, I noticed that my distraught father's body was already rested on the bed. Following my ill father's instructions, Brice and I quickly scooped him up, and placed pillows against his back to position him upright. My nephew and I held a fan to his face in the hope that it provided extra oxygen through his nostrils and mouth.

A few days before that darkest Sunday morning, my mom travelled to spend some time at my sister's house in Fenoarivo. We tried to call her numerous times throughout the day, but she was unreachable. My aunt directed us to a nearby physician doctor who could examine my father's health. As we waited for the doctor to arrive, the tension was palpable as his condition deteriorated.

I remember our emotional embrace as I gently lay his head upon my right arm for support. Just moments before the doctor's arrival, my father found enough energy to raise his head. He peered towards the wall clock, perhaps to acknowledge the time of his last breath.

He mentioned previously how people in his community would stare at a clock at the point of death. So, I gently laid his head on the pillow. It was my first experience of observing someone die. Brice and I were devastated.

When the doctor finally arrived along with my aunt, she examined my father and said, "I am so sorry, he is no more". I pleaded with her like a crazy man to save my father but this time out of anger she repeated "I told you, he is no more". I immediately collapsed, all of my strength was gone, my heart was torn apart. I didn't know what to do. However, our aunt gently comforted us since we were the only ones at home that morning during the incident. After she walked the doctor out to prepare the death certificate, I took a deep breath and called out to Brice. We knelt and prayed to God for strength, comfort, wisdom, and a miracle to reach my mother, brothers, and sisters' phones. After a while, Brice went outside to lock our gate to avoid any intrusion after the doctor left.

Finally, I managed to reach my sister before sharing the sad news to the rest of my family. Well, while waiting for the family to return, prayers and grief filled my mind and heart. I prayed that dad would rest in Christ and knew that one day we will surely be together again and forever more in the new Heaven and new Earth. Afterward, I started to undress father appropriately and made him wear his new suit and new pair of white socks. My mother and siblings soon arrived, one after another to join us, weeping and grieving accordingly. The death of our father was utterly unexpected. His plan on the following day (Monday) of his death was to join my mother and sister on vacation before returning home together.

As per our custom in Madagascar, we keep the corpse at home for a few days until the day of the funeral. We kept his corpse at home for a week due to the late arrival of some of his children. Despite our grievance, I thanked God for everything. For his unconditional love, mercy, and compassion. God gave our father seventy long years. He also blessed him with his wife Hélène who is our mother and their beautiful nine children, six boys and three girls, and many grandchildren. Extended family, friends and colleagues came over to comfort, to pray and to sing for us as we normally grieved for a week.

I thank God for the gift of life. God never forsook us during our darkest moment. He still cares for our beloved mother who is now eighty-three years old. He still cares for each of our family members even though we already lost two of our brothers.

"A special gratitude to Dr Kieran Mervyn to give me this opportunity for a memory chapter of loved ones, thank you Sir".

TO GOD BE THE GLORY THEN, NOW AND FOREVER MORE

Harigo Andri
   The last born

Kieran and Faye

Finding Cara's lifeless body was the stuff of nightmares. As Harigo Andre understands, nothing can prepare you for such an experience. All contributors to this book understand the importance about being philosophical about life after experiencing significant health problems or grappling with grief. We largely believe that death is the start of something new, and how an even grander adventure awaits us all. Harigo takes great comfort that he and his brothers and father will be together again. We believe the same too.

26

CARA'S FUNERAL ANNIVERSARY

What we see is often what we dream, and vice versa

Fig. 33 Cara and Finn

We share various pictures and videos of orbs and spirit-like figures floating around our home and beyond on the *Is Mise Cara* YouTube channel @caramiamervyn and Instagram posts @caramiamervyn. What we see is often what we dream of, and vice versa. During the morning of Cara's second anniversary, I dreamt of lying in a small room with a single bed, watching large orbs drift under the door - one by one. They differed in shape, size, and colour.

One was dark, the size of a football. I then climbed out of bed and watched it transform into a girl with long dark hair, wearing a black velvet hoodie (like the one that I'd bought Cara shortly before she passed) and black leggings. Her features were hazy and not fully visible, but it was clearly our little girl Cara.

When I awoke, Faye said, "I can't believe it's two years today since Cara's funeral mass". We then reflected on my dream and discussed her cremation wearing the new black velvet hoodie. Later, as we approached the church for mass, I regretted not singing 'Black is the Colour' before the hearse drove Cara to cremation on that cold, wet January afternoon. Just then, a message arrived from my sister about her dream that same night:

Family Connections

"That's mad about the switching of the TV and all the orbs. I was just reading it on Instagram, and I thought about the 16th of January. Earlier last night I had a dream. It was in my ma's house years ago. At the end of the old long kitchen, in the cubbyhole, a man was singing 'Black is the Colour'. I ran over to him and said: "Please dedicate that song to our Cara". Then it was ringing in my ear; that's mad isn't it"?

As mentioned in the book *Is Mise Cara*, 'Black is the Colour' was sung at our wedding in Cuba and later, as we surrounded her body in the morgue in Leeds. We have countless examples of our dreams merging with reality which we'll continue to share in this book. At one stage, my dreams also seemed to interconnect with my mother's, around the same time.

Three strange men opened the door of a black taxi outside my granny Lily's home and Finn appeared in the vehicle, staring back. His eyes were alien-like, akin to the visit of what appeared to be Cara in our kitchen as described in *Is Mise Cara*. He stared menacingly back at the three men. When I called my mother the next day to explain, she instantly relayed her own dream. She'd dreamt of three evil characters in her mother's (granny Lily's) home. What were the chances of us both dreaming about three dark characters outside the same old family house on the Falls Road in Belfast?

Cara's 14th Heavenly Birthday

Cara died aged 11, just six weeks before her 12th birthday. The build-up to Cara's 14th birthday in February 2022 was tough. Lots of mixed emotions as we discussed how tall and even more beautiful, she would have been by now. I visited Cara's room the night before her birthday and could tell how the energy was already permeating. It was serene watching the orbs whiz around quite playfully.

After a few seconds of recording the activity on my phone, one large feather-like orb flew past and headed towards my feet (see *Is Mise Cara* Instagram page @caramiamervyn). I spent a few minutes searching on the floor for what seemed like a large white feather but couldn't find it. Laughing at myself for even checking, I knew Cara would be cracking up at me. Cara's Granda David remarked after watching the video clip that it was so vivid, that it seemed like someone had thrown a handkerchief over my shoulder.

Later, Faye and I created a small charity leaflet for Brendan at the York Irish Association. Upon uploading the picture to Gmail, we noticed that it was placed inside a zip file with the words: "Do something that your Future Self will thank you for". We were amazed but not surprised. It reminded us of another of Cara's letters found after she died when she wrote a message to her 'Future Self'.

The York Irish Foundation and Leeds Irish Centre are kindly supporting our charity work through sales of *Is Mise Cara: Orbs, Souls and Holy Ghosts*. We toasted Cara's life later that evening before having a relatively early night in preparation for Cara's memorial mass at St Mary's Church in Horsforth. But we all experienced different things during the night.

The birds sang outside Cara's window in the early hours, which felt serene. Faye noticed a blue-purple shining orb dance around in the darkness of the landing. She also heard some foxes being loud and playful outside the window. When Finn woke, the first thing he asked was,

'Who was singing the lullaby'? and 'Where did it come from'?
We told him that his big sister was looking out for him.

I shared Cara's Second Anniversary Mass time with friends and family and arranged to meet everyone outside the church at 12.00 lunchtime. However, my heart sank as we pulled up outside the church and noticed everyone queueing in the lashing rain. The doors were shut! The mass was scheduled for earlier that morning; I gave everyone the wrong time. I was mortified and apologised profoundly, but we laughed about it later and knew that Cara would have done so too.

27

CAMPBELL CLARK (LEEDS)

by Sandra Clark in memory of her husband, Campbell

"Thank you; you have given me strength when I needed it most. You are true friends. We can tell you lots of things that have happened to us over the years. When my dad died, I put a red rose in his coffin with him. Many years later, a friend who is also a clairvoyant said to me that "your dad has just said thank you for the rose you gave him" (Sandra Clark)

Fig. 34 Campbell

Our neighbour and friend Sandra Clark lost her husband Campbell in 2020. We often described Campbell and Sandra as like Guardian Angels. Often waiting to meet and greet Cara on her return from school. Sandra recently mentioned:

"I used to love watching Cara, Faye, and Finn come down the road laughing. At times, I imagine Cara all in pink, linking arms with her mum; she was so pretty".

Sandra and Campbell gifted Cara rosary beads after hearing of the brain tumour diagnosis and prayed often for her. When Cara passed, they presented us with a rose bush. We often capture activity around the plant and have an interesting picture showing a strand of light stemming from the sky to the plant.

They were both devastated at Cara's loss, and we were likewise saddened to hear about the passing of Campbell who was always jovial and kind-hearted. Sandra also mentioned how her young granddaughter was playing with dolls when Sandra asked what her name was, and the child remarked it was the 'Cara Doll' Fairy.

Sandra mentioned how she'd burst her appendix as a young lady and checked herself out of the hospital straight after the operation because she knew that her mother was gravely ill. Sandra was so sick that her fresh stitches burst as she tried to move her mother onto the sofa. Both lay down together. Looking past her mother at the end of the couch, Sandra recalled how she witnessed her deceased younger brother. She begged her brother not to take her mum, but sadly her mother passed away. Sandra also mentioned:

"Our priest, Father Power, who once lived near us when I was little, brought me some Shamrock back from Ireland. It was my pride and joy for years. He came to our house every day even though we were Church of England. My mam loved him. He played monopoly with us and would give us money. Just mentioning Shamrock brought back all those memories. He was going to take my 15-year-old brother to Lourdes and had holy water and a medallion sent from Lourdes for Stuart's journey, but Stuart died three weeks before he was due to go. We adored Father Power XXX."

Sandra also described some supernatural and paranormal experiences with family and friends in Durham.

- We lived in a very big old house, and saw, heard, and felt lots of things. In Glenside, I was terrified of the house and always thought a Victorian lady was around me constantly.
- Gill (Sandra's sister) is hearing lots of people talking in her house and knocking on the door when there is no one there.
- The night before we were told about my auntie collapsing, Gill, whose garden is huge, heard what sounded like a truck coming up her drive. She rushed outside but there was nothing in the drive. Later, there was banging on her door again but no one was there so she knew something was about to happen, which it did.
- This always happens to Gill 'when something is about to happen'.
- Leo (Sandra's grandson) sees a lot of things. He said the snowcat lies on his bed—Shaun's (Sandra's son) cat. Snowball and Snowflake both died aged 22 years, not long after Leo was born.

We now provide a snapshot of Sandra's recent correspondence and some of her family and friend's experiences of the afterlife.

- My two grandsons, Leo the eldest - talks of his grandad constantly. Last Sunday he was on our bed playing and said: "I can smell my granddad". The bedding is washed every week.
- It is amazing. Just yesterday, my niece, Nardia, called to see me for the first time since December. We were very upset being a close family. It was Gill's daughter. We just sat in the garage. When Nardia left, I walked into the dining room, where a large white feather was in the middle of the table. We are all getting so much love and messages.
- I keep finding his things round the house which were never there. I get

- so many signs from Campbell; I know he is here with me.
- My four-year-old great niece called with her mum. And when preparing to leave for home, asked "why did Uncle Campbell have to go to Jesus? I can see it makes Auntie Sandra sad and lonely".
- One of the images I saw looked like a face when I photographed Campbells flowers. I will send it.
- Three days ago, I got on the scales and as normal it said 13 stone, 3.5lb. I knew I didn't weigh that, so I tried again, and my weight came up. The next day the same happened. It was later I realised that was Campbell's weight just before he died because he had lost so much weight.

Kieran and Faye

One Saturday afternoon in 2021, we received a WhatsApp message from my sister Carla. It was a Lorna Byrne six-minute prayer video. After approximately two minutes and thirty seconds, Faye spotted a white image on the opposite wall. She jumped and pointed, but I didn't immediately notice. So, I decided to replay the video on my phone and glanced at the time the image appeared to Faye. And there it was. I'd describe it as a dull white fuzzy-shaped human outline without specific features. But the head and shoulders were visible. It was an incredible sight from less than three yards away. We were both elated because it once again confirmed what we already knew about Lorna Byrne, who we refer to as a living Saint. It felt like powerful energies were protecting the house.

> *The next day we walked to Sandra's home to drop off a copy of Is Mise Cara. After initial greetings and checking up on her, she immediately mentioned an incident in her bedroom. While getting changed, she looked up to see a large white human-like image drift across her bedroom. She knew in a heartbeat that it was Campbell. We knew that these integrated spiritual experiences were happening for a reason. I then showed Sandra*

my WhatsApp message to Lorna Byrne's daughter Pearl from the day before. It referred to our own experience with the white images. What were the chances of both seeing white floating images on consecutive days?

Whistler

Another example of our conscious observations being intertwined with the unconscious, was when I awoke early on a January morning to tell Faye about an uneasy dream where the dark side had once again lurked. She immediately mentioned how she woke during the night to the sound of something physically located in the bedroom.

Faye described how she observed our (me and Finn's) breathing patterns while trying to figure out the location of the noise. It soon dawned that it was neither of us. Someone was nearby, sounding breathy and whistling as it moved. She wasn't scared but was adamant that a fourth person was there amongst us.

Faye then reflected on an uncomfortable dream that woke her, where we'd ordered a large Chinese takeaway meal at her parents' house in Leeds, and how filth suddenly permeated every room. And how frantically we tried to clean the house before the food arrived. It seemed like a battle of wills, where the filth was winning no matter how much we tried to clean up. I then shared my own dream where I attended a Lorna Byrne (Spiritual Messenger and internationally bestseller author) event at a large hotel. How I kneeled and gave Lorna a copy of her own prayer book 'Prayers from the Heart'.

"Byrne gives hope and a sense of peace; something that the Church, in many instances, has been unable to do for a long time." — The Times.

"Nobody is going to argue with her underlying message of love and

compassion and forgiveness and her hopes for 'peace among nations and peace in families'. Spending time with her is both challenging and inspirational". — Irish Times

Faye mentioned another dream where she took a bottle of holy water sent by my aunt Mena and sprayed it around the house. That bottle had sat unused next to Cara's seat at the dining room table for over a year. A definite increase in paranormal activity resulted in lots of faces popping up in the living room, so I waited until Faye took Finn to bed before spraying positive energy around the walls. I didn't mention the holy water bottle and placed it back in the same location, so the chances of Faye then dreaming of the same holy water bottle that I had just used was something else.

28

RECOGNITION FROM THE CHURCH

Fig. 35 Father Emmanuel witnessed the supernatural and paranormal activity in our home and plays a key role in Is Mise Cara.

RECOGNITION FROM THE CHURCH

Many bizarre 'events' have occurred since Cara passed, which led us to seek wider perspectives from people of all faiths and cultures. Lorna Byrne has been an incredible source of love and support for our family. She helped to answer some of the questions around e.g., why multitudes of spirits, souls, and orbs began to appear at a time of grief and why they continue to reveal themselves (See Lorna's chapters in *Is Mise Cara*). We are glad to have our local Nigerian priest Father Emmanuel, and support from the Catholic Church in Knaresborough that we often visited for prayers before Cara passed.

The small chapel 'Our Lady of the Cragg' was excavated by a stonemason (John the Mason). This was offered as a gift to the Virgin Mary for saving his son. The boy somehow survived a significant rock fall during the quarrying of stone, and his father attributed the intervention to a miracle from the 'Mother of God'. We visited the chapel several times after Cara's brainstem tumour diagnosis. On one occasion, whilst praying at the desolate outdoor altar with Cara, Faye, and Finn, we were startled to hear a large rock falling from above and crashing to the ground beside us. It felt like a sign that someone, somewhere needed prayers. We are now aware that rocks occasionally fall around that area. However, it was the timing of the rock fall which we found interesting.

Lorna Byrne was pleasantly surprised to hear members of the Catholic Church, including Father Emmanuel and the Chapel of Our Lady of the Crag in Knaresborough, recognised our book. The treasurers added this statement to their church website:

BOOK COMMEMORATES CHILD VISITOR TO CRAG

Little Cara Mervyn used to visit the Chapel with her family, parents Kieran and Faye, and younger brother Finn. Tragically, Cara died from a brain tumour in the early hours of the 29th December 2019 at the age of 11. Catholics Kieran and Faye, originally from Belfast and now living in Leeds, have written a book that remembers Cara, celebrates her short life, and chronicles the many supernatural experiences that they have had after her death, reassuring them of her after-life existence[vii]

29

TERRY J. BOYLE (CANADA)

Fig. 36 Terry (RIP) graduating at University of Roehampton, London (1999)

TERRY J. BOYLE (CANADA)

As Terry Boyle (RIP) often said, each story of loss is contextually different e.g., time, location, and circumstance but the outcomes are always the same.

Terry was one of my top master's students who passed away in 2020. He trained for the priesthood for several years before deciding against it. He married and had three children. One of which died tragically.

Terry found Amy-Lyns's lifeless body and having known and met Cara, knew what we were going through. Terry provided amazing spiritual guidance and helped us to cope with the supernatural activity in his own unique and humorous way.

Terry occasionally appears to us both in vivid dreams. It feels like he's trying to share messages from the spirit world.

30

THE RING AT CLONARD MONASTERY

I received a call from my sister Carla shortly after Faye had texted my cousin Gavin's wife, Karen in Belfast. Karen had been sharing the news about Gavin's mum Phyllis' ill health. Carla mentioned how she had been in a large empty church (Clonard Monastery) praying when she found a beautiful ring on the floor.

Moments later, Phyllis and her husband John (my aunt and uncle) appeared, looking distressed. They were frantically looking for a ring that Phyllis had lost. What were the chances of their niece finding the ring at that point in time? Perhaps there were messages from the clan on the other side to pray for Phyllis? Karen has also experienced signs after losing her two boys in tragic circumstances.

On Mother's Day 2022, we visited York and sat in the park outside the large catholic cathedral. We watched a single white dove circle continuously before returning to the rooftop of the church. It returned every few minutes, circling us before returning. At one point, it stopped dead in its tracks about 10 feet away and Finn walked toward it.

It flew off, but I decided to stroll over to the spot where it sat momentarily. Sure enough, it had left a large, pure white feather. I handed it to Faye and joked how Cara wasn't going to miss another Mother's Day without leaving a gift.

Faith of the Gypsies

Cara knew that the World Champion boxer Tyson Fury's parents were Irish (North and South) and how he championed his people and provided a voice for the excluded. Travelers are often vilified in the press. Tyson had his own battles and courageously faced this head-on.

He was similar to Cara in many ways who had her own issues with mental health and low self-esteem, and never felt like one of the 'cool kids' as she often said. Such a funny and thoughtful wee woman who brought many laughs to people's lives, just like Tyson.

My mother talks glowingly of the gypsy community and how they would arrive at a chapel on the Falls Road in their dozens each week, dressed in sharp suits and nice dresses, in good time for mass. And how devout they were as there wasn't a peep as they silently prayed. She'd often say: "Their faith would put many people to shame". People are much less spiritually tolerant these days.

Face on Television

Lots of strange occurrences have taken place. As my mother and sister Carla prayed the rosary, the unmistakable picture of Our Lord Jesus Christ floated across the blank television screen. Not believing her eyes, she blinked and continued to pray – and the same figure floated again back across the screen

– slowly but surely.

My sister Carla is devout and prays a lot. One night when praying with my mother, she broke into hysterics laughing. She couldn't stop and was told off by my mother for being disrespectful. Carla mentioned how she couldn't help herself. A picture of a large gorilla with protruding teeth appeared in her mind's eye and disturbed her prayers. It's happened on other occasions and she's aware that someone somewhere hates prayers.

31

NOTE FROM GRANNY MARIE (IRELAND)

by Marie Mervyn

Fig. 37 Cara and her mum in Leeds

To have had a special 'Angel' like our granddaughter Cara Mia was such a blessing. Cara was so full of life yet so full of love. She always had the biggest smile on her face. Was at her happiest in Belfast along with her big and wee cousins, they loved her dearly and she loved them right back. I was so proud of Cara for having such great faith in God. She recited the Hail Mary in Irish - something her daddy taught her from a very young age.

NOTE FROM GRANNY MARIE (IRELAND)

Recently I was in Ballycastle, walking through Leafy Avenue surrounded by a few large Cherry Blossom Trees. Upon my path I noticed petals laying on the ground after bad weather the night before. I thought of Cara in her lovely blue checked summer dress with her mum Faye after collecting her from school. Such a beautiful picture that sits in her home in Leeds.

With Cara on my mind, I gently whispered to her to keep us safe and guide us in life, especially her mummy, daddy, and little brother Finn. Just after Cara passed, I planted a white rose bush in the garden of our home. Often a beautiful white butterfly would roam around the park, or a little bird would sit on the fence, chirping away happily. I would tell the other young grandchildren to be good and not mess about as Cara is watching over them all and was reminding us through the signs to be nice to one another.

In the strangest places of our home, we would come across little white feathers or see a quick blue spark, especially when praying with my youngest daughter Carla. I do believe this is a sign from Cara that she's at peace. God had better plans for her, he took her out of her sufferings and took her home.

Well, Cara I just want to thank God for letting us have you as our beautiful granddaughter. I and your granda, Paddy, are so proud of you kid. I still have the wee silver angel you bought me in Leeds years ago. I always keep it safe in the Christmas crib. We have a million happy memories to treasure, but my favourite ones are the great times we had on our Holidays in Lanzarote, Majorca, Donegal Ireland, and Leeds.

I know you loved coming to Belfast meeting up with all your crazy cousins and the large family of aunts and uncles and having great fun. Cara, you give us all beautiful memories. So, until we meet again Cara, rest in God's peace, always loved and missed by us all.

God Bless, Love Granny Marie and Granda Paddy xxx

32

TAYA (LEEDS)

by Sophia McCourt in memory of daughter, Taya-Louise

This late addition to our book came from Sophia, the mother of Finn's friend from primary school in Leeds. Sophia read about Cara and shared her own experiences with Faye, below.

When I was pregnant with Taya-Louise everything was fine until I went for my 20-week scan. They told me that she had a heart defect where she only had two Chambers and one tube, and the tube was also getting blocked. Her heart was also on the wrong side and a few other organs were in the wrong place. She was surviving because she was living off me. They told me that if she survived birth, she would need open-heart surgery as soon as she was born. And that if she did survive, she would have many more surgeries and probably wouldn't live a long life.

And going on to have other children we would all have to watch her die. Taya didn't survive past 30 weeks, her tube had blocked, and she passed away while I was carrying her. I gave birth to her, and she looked like a beautiful little girl just sleeping.

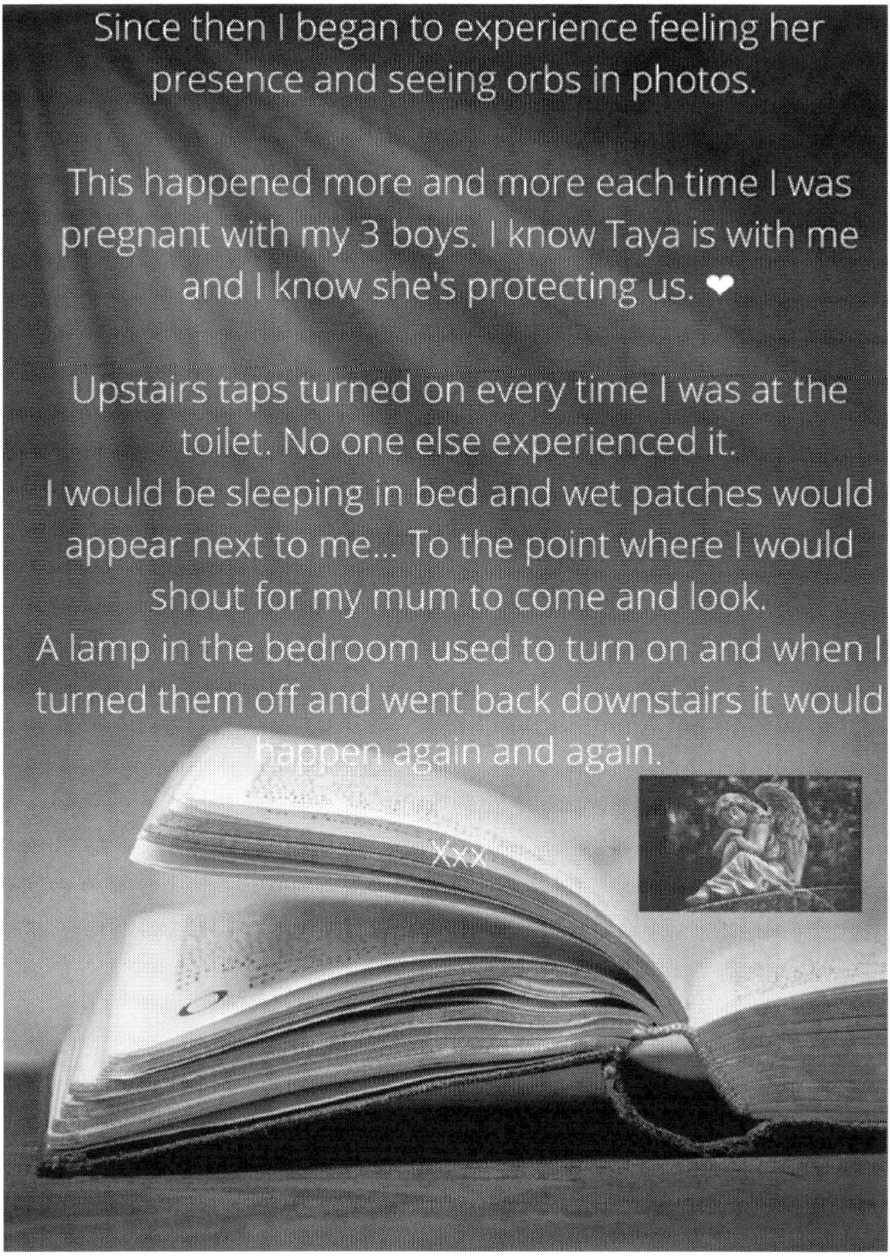

Since then I began to experience feeling her presence and seeing orbs in photos.

This happened more and more each time I was pregnant with my 3 boys. I know Taya is with me and I know she's protecting us. ♥

Upstairs taps turned on every time I was at the toilet. No one else experienced it.
I would be sleeping in bed and wet patches would appear next to me... To the point where I would shout for my mum to come and look.
A lamp in the bedroom used to turn on and when I turned them off and went back downstairs it would happen again and again.

xxx

Fig. 39 Tanya's (RIP) Mother, Sophia

33

VJOLLCA'S DAD (KOSOVAR-ALBANIAN)

"Many synchronicities involve a thing or person you've just been thinking about. And then suddenly you either meet this person, or it becomes a topic of mentioning with others".

I am very thankful for the opportunity to share my perspective on synchronicities. I am a Kosovar-Albanian living in my home country who has lost many members of our extended family at a very young age, including my father. He died at 52 after suffering from heart disease for more than 13 years and was the youngest of five brothers and a sister, who also died around the same age as him.

I have not considered the spiritual connection to synchronicity. Or at least I did not pay much attention to it until reading the book 'Is Mise Cara: Orbs, Souls and Holy Ghosts'. This reading enabled me to connect the dots of what happened, which I now see more clearly.

My father was an ordinary citizen of my home country. He lived a simple life with a regular job at a public company. Nothing too special about it. He was happily married to my mother (now 75 years old and only 47 when my

VJOLLCA'S DAD (KOSOVAR-ALBANIAN)

dad passed away) with four kids. He spent most of his time in the hospital, especially in winter. So, we were raised by my mother and him in the distance.

Vyollca's Dad

VJOLLCA'S DAD (KOSOVAR-ALBANIAN)

It was the 2nd of August, 1994, two days before my father passed away in the hospital on the 4th of August. I was in the kitchen studying and thought I heard him calling:

"Vjollca, my darling, can you hear me? No matter what, you keep studying."

At that moment, I thought he had returned from the hospital and was entering the room. Simultaneously, as I ran towards the door for a hug, a loud breaking noise was audible from the kitchen.

After approaching the entrance door and noticing no one around, I entered the kitchen to see shards of glass from the stove scattered around the floor. The pressure of the break was so big that it filled the entire room with small glass pieces.

A few hours later, we received a phone call from the hospital to say my father was in the intensive care unit as his health deteriorated. Two days after he passed away and three months later, I graduated from the University.

Synchronicity can come in other forms, too. Back to my father. As I mentioned, he passed away on the 4th of August 1994. On each anniversary of his passing, I visit his grave and spend some time-sharing family updates. It still feels therapeutic talking to him in detail about my concerns, just like I did when he was alive.

One day, I was in my room, where I kept a big picture of him hanging on the wall, and I was just lost in my thoughts. Whilst looking at the picture, it seemed like his lips moved to say the 4th is approaching.

When it comes to synchronicities, I often feel Deja Vu. Here is an example of what I mean:

I may be sitting in a room with my family or at a bar with my friends, just conversing. And in my head, I'd have this thought of a sentence of a discussion point that may come up next. And at that moment, someone involved in this discussion says the very sentence or a discussion point.

Many synchronicities involve a thing or person you've just been thinking about. And then suddenly you either meet this person, or it becomes a topic of mentioning with others.

I travel a lot for the job, but I commute daily. One day, when driving to work, I suddenly started thinking of the way I had shared my university work with a colleague from whom I had not heard for a long time. We had a great time together during our studies. She'd been my 'crying shoulder' when my dad passed away, so I started wondering about her whereabouts.

Just as this thought was in my head, the radio announced that my colleague had just been appointed the deputy minister of the Kosovo Government.

Synchronicities are a way to show love and compassion and show that things happen for a reason. They might look like a coincidence, but they show a relation to the human brain and our role as human beings, potentially supporting our thinking and actions.

34

AALIYAH – HIGHEST POWER (IRELAND)

By Lauren McCormick

"I remember when I picked you to be my mammy in heaven".

Aaliyah (meaning highest power) was born on 30th January 2015. I was 18, had just graduated from college and was terrified to bring this new baby into the world at such a young age. We wanted to keep the gender a surprise, so when we had seen this perfectly beautiful little girl, all my worries and fears melted away.

Aaliyah (Dublin, Ireland)

I knew from the moment Aaliyah was born she was special. Of course, every child is precious and special but deep down I could feel there was something different about her.

Thanks to my mother, Sharon, I have always been very spiritual and believe in God and all his angel's work. From as young as I can remember, she has told me stories about angels and their power. I remember, as a child, always seeing spirits inside our home. I was never frightened, just always fascinated. My Mam had told me to 'not be afraid as they wouldn't want me to be frightened'; they wanted to say hello. As well as seeing these spirits, I could hear them; they would call out my name. As I became older, I began not to see these spirits any longer, but to this day, I still hear them.

AALIYAH – HIGHEST POWER (IRELAND)

This is why Aaliyah was so special; she could also see and hear angels from a very young age. When she was around three or four, I remember we were chatting in bed, and she said to me out of the blue, "Mammy, I remember when I picked you to be my mammy in heaven".

I paused and said, "Really; can you tell me more?". She explained that she remembers many children with her in heaven and that the angel said its time for you to pick out your Mammy. She said she had seen me. She described how I was out somewhere, and then she said, "I want it to be her!". I asked, "and what happened then?" She said, "the angel took me back to the other children." I was speechless.

So, from a very early age, Aaliyah was connected spiritually. She would always have vivid dreams and, throughout the years, tell us various stories like the one she remembers of her in heaven.

Aaliyah was a funny, sweet, kind-hearted, happy, amazing little girl. She was wise beyond her years and had the most amazing aura about her. So, when we discovered she had a brain tumour in July of 2021 at six years old, our whole world turned upside down. She never had any health issues and was always a healthy child. We found out through a biopsy she had a high-grade Brainstem Glioma, also known as Diffuse Intrinsic Pontine Glioma (DIPG). This is a fast-growing, aggressive malignant brain tumour. We were told Radiation and Chemotherapy were to keep this monster at bay and that Aaliyah's Cancer was terminal. We were looking at 6-9 months after diagnosis but were told she would be lucky to see six months.

Karl and I's minds were in overdrive; how could our precious daughter have cancer? We were devastated that this was happening to our daughter. No child should experience cancer, but we knew there was nothing we could do but pray harder than we ever had before.

We did Radiation and Chemotherapy as planned. In fear of the future, we never stopped praying. All our family prayed, and people travelled to Lourdes and Knock (Shrine) just to light candles and have a mass said for Aaliyah. All around the world, people were praying for her. We connected with a faith healer, who would sit weekly with Aaliyah for healing sessions. Aaliyah would describe the tingling and heat from his hands as he lay them on her head. She was so relaxed and loved these healing sessions; she would focus on her breathing like in meditation, which myself and her would practise regularly.

On different occasions this year, Aaliyah saw what she described as her Guardian Angel on her own, which she decided to call 'Gabby'. Both times she had just woken up and seen this white light appearing out of nowhere. She said she just watched it change from a white orb to eventually become an angel. She described how it was beautiful and big in size. She said she had no wings but was all white and almost translucent.

One of the times when she screamed out for me, I thought she'd fallen or something, so I ran in, and she was just sitting there with a shocked look on her face. She then told me what she had seen. I told her how beautiful and special that was, that her angel was letting her know she was always with her and minding her.

Aaliyah, after radiation, did exceptionally well, better than doctors thought she would, and she returned to school in September. She attended every single day for more than nine months, something no one thought would happen. Throughout her cancer journey, she remained Funny, Positive, and Happy and always was described by people that she was 'never without a smile. We made so many amazing memories and did not let cancer take over our life. Sadly, our beloved daughter Aaliyah passed away on 18/08/2022, one year, one month & one day after diagnosis, an Angel number 111 that we always came across in our life.

She passed away so perfectly and peacefully in her Mammy and

Daddy's arms and surrounded by her loved ones. Things happened very quickly towards the end; we were told she had maybe five months left, but things took a turn. I prayed to God and told him that as much as I wanted Aaliyah here, I did not want her suffering anymore. And I feel he heard me. Thankfully she did not suffer as we thought she would. When I knew the time was coming for Aaliyah to depart, I lay beside her and repeatedly told her how much we loved her, how proud we were of her and that it was okay to rest now.

I whispered in her ear to give me signs of what she loved most, *sunsets, rainbows and butterflies*. Whilst we were in the hospital, everyone had cleared the room. It was just Aaliyah and me; she was peaceful and beautifully still. I told her, "Please let mammy know somehow that you are okay". Two seconds later, Karl returned to the room; he handed me a little bag and said the nurse had told me to give this to you. I opened it, and it was two beautiful crystal butterflies.

One was for Aaliyah to hold forever in her hand, and the other was for us to have so that we would always be connected. I gasped and told Karl that I had just asked her for a sign; he couldn't believe it. I knew it was her way of letting us know she was okay.

From that day forward, we were met with the most beautiful signs from Aaliyah. For eight days after her passing, we were met with the most amazing sunsets, rainbows and butterflies. The sun shined every single day with no rain present. Magnificent rainbows appeared almost constantly. There were people all over the world sending us videos and pictures of all these signs and saying how it was our girl, letting everyone know she was happy and whole again.

The day we laid her to rest was a beautiful day. So many people came who supported us throughout our journey. When the day was almost done, we were at the afters of her funeral when one of my friends had called us all outside. In the sky was this magnificent huge rainbow right above the pub. Strangers in the street stopped to take pictures; people who were just dining inside came out to just stare at this rainbow. The colours in which it showed were like nothing any of us had seen before.

The sky was orange and pink, it beamed such radiance, we all stood there in awe. I knew that was her way of letting us know she is still with us.

A few days after, we visited Aaliyah's grave. It was a beautiful, calm sunny day. Through my sunglasses, I could see a rainbow appearing in the distance. I thought, 'there's been no rain, so how is there a rainbow on this sunny day'? Karl had been sitting down praying to Aaliyah when he saw not one, but two rainbows appear. These weren't regular rainbows; we could only describe them as light beams. They weren't shaped like a regular rainbow but just two beams of rainbow light in this beautiful blue sky. An old man beside us visiting a loved one overheard us and couldn't believe what he saw either. We thanked Aaliyah for all these amazing reassuring signs. I said from day one, she was special, and now she is even more powerful in heaven.

We have visited Aaliyah every day since her passing. There is a lovely calmness at the spot where she now rests, and we love to just sit and chat. One day recently, we were very upset because we missed her so much. We asked Aaliyah for a sign, and low and behold, Karl said, 'Lauren, look at that cloud in the sky. As clear as anything in the big blue sky was a cloud in the shape of an "A" right over her grave. I took out my phone and shared the pictures with family and friends. Everyone was shocked; they knew Aaliyah was capable of these amazing signs, but this huge A was unexplainable. We just laughed; how amazing was this? I joked and said to Karl thank God for cameras because no one would believe us!

We have been given many amazing signs from Aaliyah; not just us but family, friends, and even strangers have reached out to tell us about these signs. When we reflect on Aaliyah's battle with cancer, we always pray for a cure, something to heal her. I always prayed to my Guardian Angel to help guide me. To be the best mother to Aaliyah and help me make the right decisions regarding her treatments. It's only now we realise how well Aaliyah remained before her death.

She wasn't this terminally ill child; she lived every day to the full. All our pictures and videos show her being a loving, carefree child. We believe that she could live a normal life through the power of prayer. Most children with DIPG are very sick; it affects the brainstem, where all the most vital body functions are located. Many children with this diagnosis were wheelchair-bound and could not walk or talk.

It was only in the last couple of weeks in the lead-up to Aaliyah's passing that her mobility became impaired. Aaliyah was extremely blessed to have little-to-no side effects throughout her year. There were unexplained things that baffled a few doctors with Aaliyah. For instance, one MRI scan showed 20% shrinkage in her tumour, and one of the doctors explained how this was "shocking and impossible" as we had done radiation so long ago. Another was when Aaliyah was first diagnosed; she did not need a shunt. This procedure entails a shunt placed in the brain to drain fluid from a build-up of pressure from the tumour. It was only after joining this DIPG group that I learned Aaliyah was the only child I came across that did not need one. In this group, there are people from all over the world, and when I shared with other parents that she did not need one, they were stunned. Every hospital visit, we were asked, 'has she a shunt? Yes? When we would reply 'no', they would look baffled!

Many things through Aaliyah's journey did not add up. Statistically, she should have been very sick but was not. I believe this was due to the power of prayer. Every night in bed, we prayed with Aaliyah, and it got to the stage where she would just begin to pray.

The one prayer we always recited was Lorna Byrnes's prayer, "Prayer of thy healing Angels" [viii]. This prayer is so powerful. It is a prayer carried from God by Michael thy Archangel. It has been a staple prayer for many years in our family.

My mother, Sharon, came across Lorna Byrnes' books many years ago and passed them on to my sisters and me. We believe this prayer had the power to help Aaliyah remain so well. We continued to pray for a cure, but that wasn't in HIS plan. Instead, he made her well enough so we could make beautiful memories and cherish every second we had with her.
She outlived the lifespan doctors had forecasted. Aaliyah made history and became the first child in Ireland to travel to France and receive a trial drug called Onc201. This treatment was something Karl and I had spent many sleepless nights researching about. That will hopefully pave the way for the children diagnosed with DIPG/DMG after Aaliyah.

Life has a funny way of working out. I believe in God's timing and that everything happens exactly how it's supposed to. We may not see why now, but I think it will hopefully make sense someday. I knew Aaliyah was special the minute she was born. Now we have a real Angel watching us every day.

35

SUMMARY ~ SIGNS FROM CARA AND BEYOND

In Signs from Cara and Beyond: Messages from the Spirit World, **we discussed the loss of our daughter Cara and shared supernatural and paranormal experiences that emerged afterward.**

It includes uplifting, real-life stories from several families experiencing direct communication and signs from their loved ones. There are contributions from families in e.g., Ireland, the UK, Nigeria, India, South Africa, Australia, the USA, and Mozambique. We hope that this book of healing will ease the pain of loss and provide optimism for the future. Readers are encouraged to keep an open mind and to use their own intuition when confronted with what appears to be messages from the other side.

We acknowledge that many of the stories in our book are vivid and complex, so we have included some light-hearted, real-life experiences of man-made coincidences.

In our first book *Is Mise Cara: Orbs, Souls and Holy Ghosts,* we described how in the months after Cara's death, positive energy emerged in our home at a time of great darkness.

We have captured photographs and videos of what we believe to be "appearances" from Cara and countless other souls.

As a family, we believed in the afterlife but didn't realise how much until after Cara passed. The phenomenon began after receiving a grief candle from the parents of a deceased child. Gradually we started seeing more, and now our house is often buzzing with energy.

We can feel and see it. For some reason, we can capture many images but decided to keep most for ourselves. We believe that Cara is saying she is in a good place.

OK, there are many grey areas with this topic. We understand that many people may not believe in the afterlife or prefer not to discuss it. Still, the experiences have helped us cope with grief. We are thankful to each of the families for reaching out and sharing similar appearances and signs. Our loved ones may reach out in their quest for closure or to provide hope and comfort to their family and friends.

We experience phenomena wherever we go. It's not just confined to our home in Leeds or our parents' home in Belfast. One recent example was in Otley Chevins woods on a roasting hot July day.

We were just five minutes away from the car park after a long walk when I noticed something circling. Within seconds, a strange energy pervaded before what sounded like a stone grinder pierced the air. I presumed that we were being attacked by a swarm of bees. Looking upwards, a T-shaped shadow floated away – back into the woods. I sensed that it was a demon.

Not wanting to worry Finn and Faye who were some yards behind me, I decided not to mention anything. Shortly afterwards, I deviated towards some trees, when Faye and Finn started screaming. "...Get away from the trees, there's a bad energy. There's something wrong".

They heard what appeared to be a screeching sound around them. I was standing next to them but didn't hear a thing. Faye said immediately, "I think it sounds like a bean-si (or bean-sidhe)".

There are various stories told about the "bean-sidhe". The "bean-sidhe" is a fairy woman. Legend says that she used to follow certain families and that a mournful cry would be heard near the house a night or two before someone died.

There are other stories about the "bean-sidhe" being seen at the river side washing clothes and singing a mournful song as she washed. It was also said that that was another sure sign of death. (Dúchas. i.e., 2022).

Finn was petrified. I didn't hear what they heard, and vice-versa. For me, it appeared to be extremely brutal energy. I felt the power of a soul some months beforehand, which was strange but not frightening. During this experience, I reached out to touch an orb and felt an ice-cold chill before something stung my hand. It felt like a jellyfish. But this was something else, on a much deeper level. How surreal, and even more so considering that this occurred after reciting Lorna Byrne's prayer to Cara in the woods.

The experience in the woods proceeded a week of strange events in July 2022. One night, I noticed what seemed like Finn and Faye snuggled in together as I visited the bathroom. Upon returning, 'Finn' was gone. I checked his room and was surprised to find him sound asleep. It seemed like Cara had made another visit to our room. The night beforehand, I awoke, sensing something in the bedroom. Looking up in the dark, a large female floated silently above my head.

Her face was particularly large as she stared peacefully downwards. I immediately turned towards the window, closed my eyes, and prayed. It didn't look sinister, and I sensed it may have been a Guardian Angel.

Another night, Faye woke to the feeling of someone climbing out of bed, so she presumed it was Finn. After sitting up, she realised that he was still sleeping alongside her. She immediately noticed a hazy white figure slowly leaving the room. Faye's convinced that the human-like appearance was Cara!

We suspect that the increase in supernatural and paranormal activity in recent weeks is related to Lorna Byrne. Magical energy seems to pervade when Lorna is in proximity (Pearl and Lorna Byrne reviewed this very book over the summer of 2022).

Fig. 38 Cara Mia (see Lorna's message from Cara below)

The scope and scale of visitors continue to confound us. The orbs remain particularly active, day and night, and we have witnessed many meaningful synchronicities (interconnections) – the purpose of this book, Signs from Cara and Beyond.

We are eternally grateful to those who submitted chapters and photographs of their loved ones. This book recalls stories of the departed who seem to have reconnected to show that they are at ease and at peace. Their presence is frequently felt. There is much to suggest that the hereafter or afterlife differs based on the context of each soul. Those that lose a child may have a stronger spiritual connection.

We are aware of Lorna Byrne's spiritual messenger role and the negative energies that frequently test her and how she responds to that. We also see it and live it, and really don't know how we'd have coped without Lorna's intervention.

As Lorna Byrne advises, these experiences cross all religions and faiths. People regularly use labels to make sense of things. One person's experience of supernatural and paranormal activity may differ from the next. Perhaps as Charles Stevens suggests, we shouldn't try categorising or explaining. Just accept that there is much more happening than we'll ever understand.

Losing a loved one either hardens the soul or in our case – made us more open to the spirit world. Folk either become more gentle, peaceful, and loving and there can be something humbling about losing a loved one. But grief is different for everyone (See Manesha's letter to his mother below).

We agree with Lorna that the spirit world is knocking hard but not many are listening. Lorna advises us to ask God to keep negative sources away by telling it to "Go Away" and praying. Thus, demonstrating that they're not welcome. As Lorna advises, souls can do so much more in Heaven - living in the spirit world, than they can or could whilst they were alive here on this Earth. And she also said it's because they can pray directly to God and beseech to him directly on our behalf. Souls are always in the presence of God, standing in front of him, talking to him on our behalf.

Lorna advises that the veil between the worlds is thinner than we realise. She has shared some special messages which we have included in the book.

Lorna's stance is that evil spirits are unable to illuminate or make themselves bright because they are not connected to God. All angels get their light from God and souls are a part of God, a speck of light of him. Spiritual people tend to be the target of dark forces. People often see one's spirituality as a weakness. Perhaps God has made the curtain between the two worlds thinner at our home, ever since Cara travelled to Heaven. Maybe that's why we see so much activity?

Family and friends witnessed the lights flicker directly above her coffin when Cara's body lay in rest at Slater's Funeral Home. And seconds before my aunt Jean passed away; I followed an orb that appeared on my office door without a light source. It merged into one of the frequent visitors to our home. As I captured the globe on camera, my phone beeped. My sister's text said that Jean had just passed away. It just seemed like the timing was meant to be. I sent a picture of the orb to Lorna's daughter Pearl and explained what had just happened. Jean planned to send Cara to Lourdes and pay for the full trip, so we felt like Jean's soul was stopping at our home on the way to Heaven.

One of my mother's friends has had multiple lights flicker since reading *Is Mise Cara*. The Housing Executive checked the wiring, and everything is working fine. So, she laughs and says, "Cara are you winding me up again" haha.

There is a lot of negative energy lingering in the world right now. Lorna asks us to pray to God to cleanse the world and fill it with love. Lorna refers explicitly and implicitly to a race to save humanity which is on multiple paths to destruction. The angels and Lorna are operating in tandem to pull people back from the brink. In prayer, our souls and body are closer - intertwined.

36

IS MISE CARA BRAIN DISEASE FOUNDATION

Fig. 40 Congratulations note from Nigerian Ambassador to Ireland.

The Is Mise Cara Brain Disease Foundation was registered in November 2022). Brain tumours result in the death of many children, young people, and adults under 40. More so than any other cancer, which is a damning statistic. Since national cancer spending records began in 2002, the government invested <£700 million (£680m) in breast cancer research compared to £96m on brain tumours. A recent UK parliamentary motion illustrated this disparity of £35m per year over 17 years.

Unfortunately, as of 2022, brain tumour research spending continued to receive £35m per year less over the last four years. Five-year survival for breast and prostate cancer is greater than 70%, leukaemia more than 40%, yet 12% for brain tumours. Approximately 1% of national spending on cancer research went to the study of brain tumours. The only way to improve outcomes and reduce deaths is to invest in research that will help find a cure.

Written evidence from Brain Tumour Research (BCCR0006) in April 2021 relating to questions on brain tumours and childhood cancer research found significant flaws with the current rate of spend. Patients and families expect a bleak future.

"It could take up to 100 years for brain cancer to catch up with developments in other diseases and for a cure to be found. Research into brain tumours must not be left behind – the nation needs to Level Up and invest at least £35 million a year if we are to find a cure for brain tumours in the next 20 years".

Many thanks to everyone who purchased our first book called *Is Mise Cara* ('I am Cara' in Irish). Our royalties supported brain disease charities in the UK (and will do Nigeria in 2023). The first book is available from various platforms, e.g., https://books2read.com/ismisecara and www.carabraindiseasefoundation.com

Thanks to everyone who donated further in memory of Cara. Jennie

Castlehouse believes Cara guided her through a marathon, particularly the final, challenging seven miles. She wrote:

"London Marathon Done!!! Just Believe. This was for You, Cara XXX"
We nominated Yorkshire Brain Tumour Charity (YBTC) to receive the £2,000 raised by Jennie. YBTC also received royalties from our first book sales, Cara's funeral donations, and magazine fees for the *Is Mise Cara* story.

We are also planning the translation of *Is Mise Cara* and the current book *Signs from Cara and Beyond* into Spanish, Arabic, Mandarin, and Irish languages – with more to follow.

All royalties will be donated to the Is Mise Cara Brain Disease Foundation. Our mission is to provide respite and grants for patients and their families.

Please continue to support the Is Mise Cara Brain Disease Foundation by leaving an honest book review on Amazon. That would be greatly appreciated.

We leave you with Lorna Byrne's assertion that:

"Your soul is perfect; when your soul is free of your body it can travel through the universe to places you could never even imagine. How can I help you to understand how wonderful this feeling is? There is no way to express it; no way to tell you, unless you have experienced it yourself."

(- Lorna Byrne, Angels in My Hair p186)

37

ABOUT THE AUTHORS

Dr Kieran Patrick Mervyn (Chief Executive Officer, Is Mise Cara Brain Disease Foundation) is the Co-Director of Finncara Consulting Ltd and Visiting Fellow at London South Bank University; Senior Lecturer at the University of Law, London; and MSc Engineering Management at the University of Hull; He is also a research and management consultant in health and social care, and an evaluation and insight analyst.

Kieran has been involved in extensive research project work on Leadership and Innovation. This included working for the Northern Leadership Academy (NLA), Centre for Innovation in Health Management (CIHM) and London South Bank University (Associate), where he has evaluated the Darzi Clinical Leadership programme and the Senior Leader Degree Apprenticeship Programme. Kieran has published widely In international journals, including the Journal of the American Society for Information Science and Technology (JASIST); Information Communication and Society (ICS) and the International Journal of Leadership in Public Services (IJLPS). Kieran may be reached at ismisecara@gmail.com / ceo@carabraindiseasefoundation.com

Faye Louise Mervyn (Chief Marketing Officer, Is Mise Cara Brain Disease Foundation) graduated with a BA Hons in Sociology from Liverpool John Moores University. She has held administrative and managerial roles and is currently Project Assistant and Co-Director for Finncara Consulting Ltd. Faye may be reached at ismisecara@gmail.com

38

LETTER TO AMMA (INDIA)

Mahesh's Letter to his Mum

Amma

Dear Amma, I am missing you a lot. I don't have words to express my current feelings. I wish you were here now with me. I can tell you, a mother is irreplaceable for a child. When a mother dies, her child is no longer whole and feel always empty.

After your death, my dreams plagued me whether they were about your death or when they fooled me into thinking you were still alive. Waking up in sorrow and again remembering you were dead was the hardest point of each day.

I have felt your absence every day, every hour and minute of my life since you were stolen from me. I fell into a never-ending well of pain after you died. Depression ran in my veins alongside my blood. The blood became rough and scraped up my heart.

I was stumbling through my days due to depression. I'm not telling you this to make you upset, Amma, but to let you know how profoundly losing you affected my life. I made a lot of poor decisions. Along with me, I gave up a lot of the things you had enjoyed, but after you left, they strangely lost their importance.

I searched for many things to fill myself up. I had good friends who helped and distracted me. I had the rest of my family too who gave me love and courage. Many of them console me and give me company.

Now our home is empty without you amma. Whenever I go to your room, I remember our old days.

I shed so many tears that I frequently felt like giving up. When I explained my emptiness to others, they simply didn't understand. They had not experienced the same things that I had. Always, I could see it in their eyes. They either had sympathy for me and their eyes welled up, or they were speechless.

Missing the foods you made. no one can prepare food the way you do., Amma. You gave food to me with It is not reproducible. It's impossible, no one else has your smile. You were a super mother for me. Not everyone can say that about their mothers, I am aware of that. I was lucky to have you. Amma, you were awesome, loving, giving, and kind.

From my childhood, I'm seeing the way you struggled to manage the day-to-day requirements at home and even if you won't have, you will feed us on time. When I'm sick you continuously ask me to meet the doctor and I could see the tension on your face till I recover from the sick. You cook according to my preference and stand along with me even if I'm wrong. If I go out, you continuously call and ask where I'm and what time coming back. That time I will get angry and speak disrespectfully.

Because of me, you had to face lots of struggle and embarrassment from others. You always supported me when I ask to go out with my friends on trips. You even stood up with me and supported me even though I'm wrong in many situations. We have traveled to many places when you were healthy. All of a sudden you got a prolonged cough and went to see the doctor. The day when I came to know that you are diagnosed with Lung Cancer, I couldn't even breathe for a minute and I still remember the way I cried loudly alone in a narrow corridor of the hospital.

To reconfirm, I have taken you to another hospital as I couldn't accept the situation. Finally, we end up in 4th hospital (Lakeshore Hospital) and our doctor Anupama explained about your health conditions. At that time also you were very healthy and energetic. Sorry Amma, as per my request the doctors hid your health condition from you. I thought if you come to know about the disease that carving you, you'll become tense. I tried many ways to hide and told many lies to you because I was so concerned about your health. Six months passed away like that. Maybe God decided that my company got shut down due to operational issues so I could look after you. Because of this, I could take care of you 24/7 and could spend lots of time with you.

I could feed you, make your bath, dress up, and massage your feet likewise I could do all day-to-day care of yours. Each time when we visited the hospital, I hoped that you could return to your normal life and recover soon. But God was not with us Amma.

Cancer relapse one more time and you had to take another round of chemo. I don't know whether you came to know about your disease or hid it from me. You had to face lots of struggles at the Hospital and even many times I had to scold you for not having food. Now I'm regretting those days and moments when I behaved very roughly. I never knew that you hid your pain with you and not shown it to me as you know that I will get sad. We tried our level best and gave you all the treatment which we could Amma. But destiny didn't make any miracles for both of us Amma. I hid my pain within me and not shown it to you. The only thing I can say is that I'm the luckiest son of you that I could spend those two and half years 24/7 with you, treating you like a daughter.

Sorry, Amma during your final days I had to pray to God for your early departure as you were struggling for your breath and you couldn't respond to my words. I couldn't see you the way you slept at that time and now I'm thinking how I became selfish at that time. I wish you are there now to see me on my video call and I want to share with you my new life in London. Many times, you have asked me not to leave the country but finally, you also want to see me here but unfortunately, you couldn't see it. Honestly, if you are still alive, I'll be coming back to India and staying with you Amma. That much I'm missing you every day. Even a single day I didn't stay without thinking about you.

All my thoughts are about you and thinking about our old days. I don't have any words to express your disappearance from this world. Sometimes I console myself and saying I will meet you in heaven and I want to be your son again in my next rebirth. I still remembered the hospital days that we spent together and you were so tolerant enough for all the treatment as you too wished for a speedy recovery. I once again say sorry to you for not revealing your actual health condition that is because I didn't want to see the sadness on your face Amma.

God has given me enough strength for me on your cremation day. I never expected such courage in my life as that was the day I couldn't imagine and never wish to come. Though I have recovered from that shock, I'm still thinking about you every second Amma, and praying for you a good life in heaven. As per my knowledge, you never did a wrong thing to anyone but God has given you relief from a painful situation.

This one-page letter is not at all sufficient to write about you as you were a super mother for the three of us especially for me Amma. I badly miss your presence and it is very hard to live without you Amma. Please give me enough strength and courage Amma.

Your loving son, Mahesh

39

MARTY IMLACH (SCOTLAND)

By Marty Imlach (Brain Tumour Patient and Friend of Is Mise Cara Brain Disease Foundation)

This wee chapter might be of some interest to some, and others might not. This book will diverge the raw and powerful effects a brain tumour within my pituitary gland has had on my health and well-being. The tumour is located within the central part of my head. An area that controls all the functions of weight and hormone chemical production, like many other parts of the necessary functions we call life.

I have worked as an Engineer all my life. I've also been active and fortunate to see the world and get paid for it. I also had so many life experiences in a different culture. So as the time came to hang up the travelling bags and working clothing, I took a promotion into the office and started my new journey into management and office life. I began to notice the weight piling on. As we all do, I thought it was the change to being a desk jockey. Then the tiredness and the main warning was that I was getting sore heads and cranky (more than normal). So I took the plunge, went to the doctor, spoke to them, and was told to lose some weight, "you will be okay", etc. Well, a few months passed tried the gym and did the diets etc., to no avail. I spoke to my Liver specialist as I have another issue which is a lifelong condition.

I talked to my consultant, and he took types of blood and said he would do a check-up on all the normal stuff they test for and my thyroid, and he would be back in touch f there was an issue.

A week later, out of the blue, I received a call from the doctor for surgery; "We'd like more blood; please come in straight away". In the blood tests, they found I have very high levels of Prolactin. I was referred for an MRI of my skull and to the endocrine consultant for an emergency appointment.

From this appointment, I have prescribed a medication to which I reacted. I was removed from it ASAP and told I would be referred for a transsphenoidal procedure (through your nose).

I waited for an appointment, and then, three months later, the procedure was carried out. I was told there would be swelling around the area, and I would probably have black eyes and a couple of other things after the operation.

After the procedure, I had a few issues with being in the light. I was very photosensitive and was taken to the CAT scanner and informed I had swelling internally. It was impinging on my optic nerves; that was why I was light-sensitive. So sitting in the hospital ward in the middle of Sept with a pair of wrap-around shades, I felt like a fool! After a short period, I was advised about a potential return to the theatre to clear out the swelling if I did not react to the drugs within 48 hrs. Fortunately, it came good, and I was discharged and sent home for the recovery period at home. This recovery lasted three months, and I was back to work and started where I left my role.

You may ask why I am writing this in this book; well, I can tell you there is always hope and the medical teams that look after you are the best they can be, and you have to trust them as they have YOUR best interests at heart.
If I can survive this episode in my life, anyone can, with the love, support, and

dedication of family and medical teams. I must admit to this determination to survive. You will come through on the other side. Today I have slight issues, like the thyroid in my head does not work. I have drugs every day for it, and life goes on as usual.

I still work as an Engineer and have now moved into management and project management. With this, I took the plunge and did my Engineering master's in "Engineering management" at Hull university, where I came across the founder of the charity "Is Mise Cara Brain Disease Foundation", Dr Kieran Mervyn, a tutor for my course module. The topic of brain tumours was brought up in a webinar, and the rest is history.
I am proud to be part of this charity to give back something to everyone and use myself as living proof that a brain tumour is survivable. I am one of the unfortunate ones who are still here!

I have a good friend whose son has been diagnosed with a terminal tumour. I see the other side of the fence and what he is going through, for which I feel a heartfelt realisation of how life is precious as I am one of the lucky ones. There is still plenty of work left to be done to help with the research into this tumour and how they can be treated, and in the future, we can save them all.

40

MICHAEL MELVILLE (LIVERPOOL)

Cara is still very much with us. Every time we (my wife Becky, son George and daughter Emelia) get together with Kieran, Faye and Finn, it feels like she is in the room. Like she's sitting around the table with us. Each year, we would get together for Boxing Day. Roast dinner, football on the TV and Cara, Finn, George and Emelia entertain the family with fashion shows and magic tricks. Usually, Finn had the job as the main character or magician's assistant.

Whatever the performance, it would always involve Finn at the heart of the madness. She would direct Finn from the sidelines, laughing until her face would turn bright red. I know that Cara could be quite shy, but she was always a ball of energy when we visited. Amazingly, we are still feeling that energy now. Any scientist will tell you that energy can neither be created nor destroyed– it can only be converted from one form of energy to another.

Cara's energy manifests itself in many ways; we just need to look to find her. Recently, Kieran told me about the robin that kept appearing in his garden (robins are viewed as a symbol of visits from those we lost). We got to talking (over an incredibly hot Indian curry!) about the reasons for Cara sending these messages. I thought the answer was quite simple. It is because some of us are more receptive to the messages from those who passed over to the other side.

As long as we keep looking, Cara will let us know she is here. Kieran and Faye have often called for Cara to send them a sign; her continued contact has helped them get through unimaginable grief. Cara may be unable to mend her parents' broken hearts, but she will always be there when the pain gets too much.

Much is said about grief, especially the conventional wisdom that you 'do it alone'. This book suggests that this does not have to be the case. You can feel each family's emotional release when offering their story to others and the comfort they have taken from sharing their memories. It is also clear that each piece is written for different purposes. Not only for people reading these stories but also for families themselves to have the opportunity to speak directly to those we have lost. Letting them know that we have received their messages, that we are listening and that they will always be a part of us.

I found that those who contributed to *Signs from Cara and Beyond* did not take their time with their deceased loved ones for granted. All who contributed appeared to understand that every moment spent with our loved ones was sacred and the time together was never taken for granted. It was never just a trip to the park, not just a family holiday or having friends visiting on Boxing Day. The time spent with our loved ones that have passed was everything, every event and precious moment. The fact that these moments were transitory only makes them more beautiful. From reading the accounts offered here, it is amazing that these memories are still being created. I hope there a many more.

BIBLIOGRAPHY

[i] https://www.ranker.com/list/what-is-heaven-really-like/jacob-shelton

[ii] https://burialsandbeyond.com/2019/06/20/the-house-of-faces/

[iii] Trish MacGregor and Rob MacGregor, The 7 Secrets of Synchronicity: Your Guide to Finding Meaning in Signs Big and Small, Hay House UK, 2011.

[iv] Darby O'Gill and the Little People: https://www.imdb.com/title/tt0052722/ [Consulted online

[v] https://www.culturematters.org.uk/index.php/arts/poetry/item/3314-easter-rising-1916-mise-eire-i-am-ireland-by-padraig-pearse

[vi] https://blog.prepscholar.com/the-raven-poem-summar

[vii] http://chapelofourladyofthecrag.btck.co.uk/News

[viii] https://lornabyrne.com/2020/02/25/prayer-of-thy-healing-angels/

About the Author

Dr Kieran and Faye Mervyn wish to leave a legacy for Cara through the Is Mise Cara Brain Disease Foundation.

You can connect with me on:
- http://www.carabraindiseasefoundation.com
- https://twitter.com/MiseCara
- https://www.facebook.com/ismise.cara
- https://books2read.com/ismisecara

Subscribe to my newsletter:
- https://www.carabraindiseasefoundation.com

Also by Kieran Mervyn

Is Mise Cara is available on Amazon and via the global book link: books2read.com/ismisecara

Is Mise Cara ~ Orbs, Souls and Holy Ghosts

Is Mise Cara is the story of a charming young girl (Cara Mia Mervyn) who died of a brainstem tumour in December 2019.

Cara's death has opened a 'Pandoras Box' of bizarre paranormal and supernatural activity. Pandora's Box refers to things that are best left untouched.

But why do orbs and spirits emerge, and what are their underlying messages? The spiritual guide and international, best-selling author Lorna Byrne (Angels in my Hair) plays a central role in the book.

She advises Cara's parents on how to deal with the phenomenon by focusing on the positive energies that surround them.

These events have reinvigorated Cara's family and provided spiritual hope amidst the pain of grief.

'Is Mise Cara' book royalties are supporting global brain disease charities including the Is Mise Cara Brain Disease Foundation. www.carabraindiseasefoundation.com

Printed in Great Britain
by Amazon